D1321436

SALES & BUSINESS
LANGUAGE & BEHAVIOR

PERSUASION
ENGINEERING™

by
Richard Bandler
and
John La Valle

Meta Publications, Inc.
P.O. Box 1910, Capitola, CA 95010
(408) 464-0254 • Fax (408) 464-0517

Library of Congress Card Catalog Number: 95-076816
ISBN 0-916990-36-2

FIRST PRINTING – JULY 1996

❦ DEDICATIONS

To Paula, the most beautiful woman in the world.

— *Richard*

Dedicated to Kathleen, who gives me all of everything I can ever desire, and to John Sebastian, who teaches me what learning is all about. Together, they are who they are so I can be who I am.

— *John*

❦ *TABLE OF CONTENTS*

—READER TAKE NOTE!—

While it may seem that some of the sentence structures in this book read as grammatically incorrect, they are written for a purpose, as NLP and grammar do not necessarily share the same structure.

❧ INTRODUCTION

One Monday a few years ago, I woke up and decided that I would go out that day and buy a new car. So I went.

I walked into a car dealership and stood there for about 10 minutes waiting to buy a car. It didn't appear to me that the salesman was very busy. He was on the phone. He was leaning back with his feet up, cigarette in his hand, with a cup of coffee, laughing and joking. It didn't look to me like he was talking with a customer. I finally got his attention. I looked over at him and gave him the "Are you going to come over and help me?" look. And he gave me the "wait for me" signal. I walked out of the dealership.

I drove to a second car dealership, selling the same automobile. I walked up to the salesman on the floor and I said, "How would you like to sell a car today?" He said, "Sure." I described the car to him and I said, "Here's what I want. Here's the exact car I want. You have one out in the parking lot. I saw it before I came in. Here's what I need to know from you. I want to know the best price - I'm not going to argue about price. I need the best price and I want the keys to the car because I want to test drive the car." And he said, "Well, that's not the car you want. It's not you." I, of course looked out at the car and agreed to myself that it wasn't me because it was there and I was here. After a brief pause, I said, "Yes, that's the car I want." And he said, "No, it

isn't." And I said, "Of course, it is!" And he said, "No, it isn't."
And I said, "Yes, it is!" And he said, "You're not listening to me."
So I agreed with him, "You're right!" and I left the dealership.

I went into the next car dealership, the third one in the same
day, same kind of car. I was really motivated to buy a car that day.
I got somebody to take care of me in a short period of time (about
5 minutes). A salesman came up to me and I said to him, "Want
to sell a car today?" And he said, "Sure." I said, "Here's how you
can do it: keys to the car; best price; no kidding. I've already
shopped around. This is the car I want and you have one out in
the parking lot, the color I want and everything." He said, "I have
to tell you about the options first." I said, "I'm not interested in
the options. This is exactly what I want. I've been shopping for
months. I'm done shopping. Now I want to buy." He said, "I
can't sell you the car until I show you the options." I told him I
wasn't interested in the options because I was putting my money
under the hood. He said, "The company insists that I can't sell
you a car until I go over the options with you. I said, "You're
right. You can't sell me the car!" And I left.

I drove to the fourth dealership. I guess you can imagine how
I felt, as a customer goes. The salesman looked up, his eyes got
wide as he studied me. It was about 4 in the afternoon. I walked
in. As the guy looked at me (with that "I've just about had it
today" look), I asked him, "Do you want to sell a car today?" He
looked at me and said, "I can see you've had a rough day." And I
said, "Yeah, and I've had it. You're the last guy that I'm going to
talk to. If you can't sell me the car I want, and I'm going to make
it so easy for you, I'm not going to buy this car. I'm going to buy
some other car somewhere else." He looked at me and he said,
"What do I have to do?" I said, "Get me the best price and the keys
to the car. We're not going to haggle. And we're not going to go
back and forth on this thing. You give me the best price you can.

We're not going to haggle by talking to the boss, talking to the manager. You get one trip to the manager and come back with the best price! I already know what the list price is. I know what you bought it for. I know all that. Just give me the best price you can. If it matches what I want, and if the car handles the way I want it to, I'm going to buy the car - RIGHT NOW."

This guy is great! He turns around and says, "Here are the keys." He says, "Take the car. Take it by yourself and feel free to go on the highway with it. If it needs gas, put gas in it and bring back the receipt. By the time you get back, I will have the best price in the state for you." On my way out to test drive the car, I said, "And the papers. You can draw them up right now." And that's where I bought the car.

✹ CHAPTER ONE:
To Begin With

One of the best ways to know how best to engineer persuasion is to first notice how *you* respond as a customer. You know, others tell you to put yourself in the customer's shoes. Well, the problem is, not everybody wants to wear someone else's shoes. So that strategy isn't that great, as the saying goes. But when you're the customer, notice the processes that occur and begin to build the things into your selling model that you know work and begin to build into that model the options and choice points that you may need in order to redirect the process as it occurs. We call this part of the generative change process.

There are some good strategies out there except for one thing: they don't have the loop where the person continues to learn throughout their lives. Just because they have a strategy that works today, doesn't necessarily mean it will work tomorrow, or even next year, as variables change in the environment. I know companies that have come close to or even have failed because of their inability to *respond* to the environment. Feedback is the "breakfast of champions."

Just today, we got a call from a potential client who wants us to come in to teach our selling skills to their sales people. And we said to them, "What is it that your customers want or need? What is it that your customers buy?" And they said, "What's the difference? We're not that interested in what the customer wants. We're interested in giving our sales people selling skills so they can sell more of what we already have." And we said, "OK, we can do that. And what is it that you're customers really want from you? What is it that they buy from you? Is it your product? Your service? What is the value to your customers?" Their response: "We're not interested in that. We're interested in teaching our people to get others to buy from us." They didn't care whether or not the customer has the money. They just wanted us to teach their people how to get money from them. They're still a *potential* client of ours. I don't teach these skills if they have that kind of attitude because the skills we teach are powerful and they work. You may think, hey a buck's a buck, but with all the opportunities that are out there, we get to pick and choose our customers most of the time. We want to have customer satisfaction, not buyer's remorse. One of the most important skills is to know the difference up front because, how can you know what to do next if you don't even know where you are, like driving to Boston. If you're driving from San Francisco to Boston, how would you know where and when to turn, unless you pay attention to what's in front of you and what's going on around you.

When you're selling, we make the basic assumption that what you sell is a quality product or service and that you back up that product or service yourself. Just like anything else, when you believe in it, you will sell it. We don't care if it's an idea, product, service, or whatever. Strong beliefs are the second place to look.

We're going to cover some of the basics in this book as well as some of the advanced skills that the best of the sales people we have studied use every day. Some of the basic skills are still the best, especially for the foundation of anything you want to accomplish. So, when we combine these foundational skills with some of the up-to-date things we want you to use here, it's because we continue to find them most useful.

How we've engineered influence helps us to use a lot of examples. You know, we can do more than one thing at a time and for humans, sometimes that's difficult but I find that it's better for you if you do it that way.

The other element that we are going to be covering here is that this real sales course boils down to only a two step process. We are going to stretch it out a little bit to cover the process from the end to the beginning. But it boils down to when you *really* want to sell something.

I have a good business associate who has a group of sales people working for him, about 15, and we all got together one day for an evening after a program. I noticed that a good percentage of these men and women drove into the parking lot in some late model rather high priced cars. I said to him, "Gee Bob, you really pay your people pretty well. Either that, or they are really selling their butts off." He said, "I don't pay them that well, as far as their salaries are concerned. Some of them really work hard. They can't afford these cars. But every time one of them buys one, I smile because I know they are going to be the most motivated they can be just to keep up with the payments. I like my sales people to be a little hungry. There's nothing better to keep them moving." And so, he considers them to be self motivated. Anytime one of them starts to slack off a little, he asks them how the new car is.

What you do is you induce a wanton buying state and show them the product. Now, I got this idea when I was treating clients, because I did a lot of modeling in the field of psychotherapy, before I stopped and said "What am I doing?"

So, I modeled therapists, and therapists are pretty good sales people, especially the ones that were good. Guys like Milton Erickson, who was a great hypnotist. Actually there is a salesman who is like Milton Erickson. His name was Ben Feldman and they actually talked alike, had the same intonation pattern and it really surprised me because when I first met Milton I thought he was the weirdest thing on the earth. And, yet, he was so great because he could get people to do just about anything. I mean he had them out looking for Bojum trees in the desert. We would ask, "Why do you do that with people, Milton?" "Just to find out if you can," he said. "Just to find out if you can. Right!" I said.

And what surprised me was, first Milton was a cranky old guy and he'd just sit there, and go into a deep trance. And when I met Ben Feldman the thing was he had exactly the same tonality. Only, he had this book that he brought around with him and when he opened up to the first page, the first page was filled with money, loosely shoved under plastic so when he opened it, it would kind of come out and fly around. That was his step number one, **get attention**. Then he'd turn the page and there was a picture right there of Ernest Hemingway and he'd look at them and he'd go, "Ernest Hemingway is dead!" Pretty direct, huh? And you know, people would look down, and he goes, "And when Ernest Hemingway died," and he'd turn the page, "he left his family penniless, with nothing, out on the street, you know, with no life at all. Now you have a family, and you could be dead! And so people would go (ugh) and he would reach over and anchor that response.

So, what I want you to think about is, what is it that you sell? What is it that you *think* you sell? Some responses I've gotten include: "Career management for women." "We sell piece of mind." "Nice furniture. Office furniture." "Support for managers going through change." "Alternative health products." "Business insurance." "New homes." "Advocacy." "Jobs. I sell people." (I thought this was illegal). "Graphic solutions." "Financial services." And then there is the ever popular response, "Myself" (also illegal in most states in the U.S.).

And the list goes on and on like this. Put all that aside. If you don't know what you *really* sell, you're wasting your time.

Take this as an example. We've conducted sales training seminars for one of the larger new home builders. And in "the recession" over the past few years, in one of those years they sold a mountain of homes. Because they understand that they don't sell homes. *They sell feelings.* They sell comfort. They sell value. They sell safety. They sell security. They sell convenience. They sell piece of mind. They sell, in some cases, life style. In other cases, they sell school systems. They sell education and they sell everything else, except houses. And they sold more homes that year because they understand that *all you sell are feelings.* Now, how you get to those feelings, how you help the customer to feel right about what it is that they want is one of the other skills we'll get to.

The other thing now is whether you believe in what you sell. Do you believe in your product or service?

The thing is that, somebody once asked me, they said "isn't NLP manipulative?" and I said, "Yeah, of course it is." I said, "But, if you are going to force somebody to do something you use the pistol training model, it works much better." The idea is, you don't use conviction as a way of manipulating somebody. What you do is, you open up the channels and make it so that you can get people's natural processes to work for you. Anybody who sells something that they don't believe in, is only going to hurt themselves in the end. They are not going to do that well. They may do well for a while, and feel clever. But then they will find themselves, worshipping volcanoes or some weird thing to make up for it. You know, it happens. The trick is to find something that you believe in. Because, to me, I believe that you need to have a foundation of product knowledge, which means you have to know what you are doing. This is something that I would like to introduce, especially into electronics stores. Places where they sell computers, it would be nice if the salesperson knew how they worked and what they did. It's recommended, that instead of having to call some 800 number to find out how the things work and wait in line and have someone speak to you in a foreign language, it would be nice if some guy in the store could actually show you how the products work.

I modeled the skills from these guys whose close ratio was 97% or higher, ouch! Now I wasn't sure if I wanted to do this project. I had to think this through and I had to make sure I was ready for this one. The thing these guys were great at is that you have to be able to build in and inoculate people against buyer's remorse. And you have to be somebody who never has to overcome objections.

We've looked at many sales courses. There are those, of course, selling the psychological approach, which, if you use, I'm sure you could cut your sales in half, just like that. It's funny, they hire us to increase their revenues. And then they spend this enormous amount of time trying to prove that what they are doing is great, but they are not happy with it. These are people who are not congruent.

But basically the idea is, in most sales, most negotiations and in most of the situations in which people do, what I call, "Persuasion Engineering™," they teach people a canned ritual approach. One approach, the trick is to use it with as many people as possible. Now even if you do pretty well, you find a good approach and your close ratio is pretty high, it still means the only way that you can make more money is by prospecting more and by spending more time. So if you are seeing a hundred people, and you are closing thirty of them, then you need to see three hundred to triple your income. Which means you need to prospect 300 people, 300% more, so usually, by the time you hit 45 or 50, you blow a fuse somewhere upstairs or in the arteries. So what happens is, you have to work so hard you go into burn out stage and you stop doing even what does work. The alternative is to do what I call being a professional, which means that you learn to identify external things and to adjust your behavior and go after the other 70%, and by the way for those of you who have been doing this for a long time, it becomes fun again. Because what happens is that anybody that you know, because all the salesman tell me all the same thing: "If somebody walks in the door, I know whether I can sell to them or not." And I say, "Well, if you know that what you are going to do is not going to work, how come you don't do something else?" They say, "Well there is nothing else that will work, nothing on the face of the earth will ever work with these people." Well, we ran a little experiment with this. I went down to a furniture store, which is out by the side of the freeway, in Louisiana, and I had these guys who had been working at this place forever, and some of these guys were quite good at what they did. People would walk in and they said they could sell them most of the time and they would close the sale. However, over 70% of the ones that walked in the door, they would go, "Oh, no! They are not going to buy anything." And sure enough they couldn't sell them anything. So I started taking those people, to find out. And I found out I could sell stuff to them. It didn't even matter what! I could sell them the guy's car out in the parking lot. If you adjust your behavior, and I also found out, that if we actually just divided them up right, so that this guy got these kind of people and these guys got this kind of people, we could increase their close ratio, just by funneling through the right guy, cause they didn't all do the same thing.

They didn't all talk the same way, they didn't all speak at the same rate and they didn't all use the same kind of nonverbal communication. Now the trick here is to realize that what ever you do right now, that works, you want to slice all of that off and know that when you finish here, you will be able to do that. What you are looking for are those clients. And we want to start out to create a change in your mind and I want to use a reference point. I want you to stop . . . and think about somebody that you have to negotiate with, or you have to sell to, or a kind of person, that when they walk in the door a voice inside your head goes, "Oh, shit," something inside of you goes (Grrrrr) and for a moment close your eyes and think of one of those people, because they are going to be your reference point. You will know here when you've learned something when you can close your eyes and imagine them. And they look like food. That deep voice always helps, when the client walks in and you look at them and you go, "Poor soul."

Now in the middle of the time that I have developed this sales training program, I actually developed it for a company and I went around and I modeled it and different things. And I discovered that there are different aspects of what it takes to be one of these people that's just dynamite. I always try these models, I'm one of these people that believes, and, in fact, when I left the "ivory tower" I was criticized for getting my hands dirty, because I liked to take all the things that I thought about and used them to make sure they worked. And my colleagues at the time thought that was disgusting. They considered that as getting your hands dirty. They are the kind of people that with pride say give me a button and I won't push it. Of course, they don't make that much money and they live in the ivory tower. They are living in think tanks right now, most of them. You'd think, think tanks would be full of wonderful things to think about, however, they're not, they're empty. I know, they tried to get me to go in them. They brought me up there and there was just a big empty building with people doing this. And I know they couldn't be thinking about much, because if they were they would be doing this. I know what happened is they went inside, they found the slide pictures, stepped inside it and were frozen in time. And I actually got to go to some of these conferences they had up there and we discussed issues and most of the time it was stuff like the shape of the table. Their ability to find things that were relevant were so far removed, that when we had luncheons, I could steal all of their food and they wouldn't know it. I would. I would go home with all of their food, you know, and then after lunch they would all be going "I'm so full." But I'd ask them questions, like, "How did you get started here?" And when they'd go inside, I'd go (Fsht), now, I can see, why I bothered.

And what we are going to do here, has to do with increasing two things. One, I found that every good person who engineered influence had first a road map, they had a way of knowing where to start, and a way of knowing when they were done. Which is particularly important, and had some kind steps along the way so that they changed from doing one kind of behavior to another. Some of them, you see most of them, spend a very short amount of time, getting people's attention, because most of these people were fairly outlandish. You know, it went from Ben Feldman with his book with all the money in it to one of these other guys with their 97% close ratio.

Selling ideas is one thing. Some of us sell products, some of us services, some of us, get to negotiate.

This is a great thing. I got to negotiate, just me, against 16 lawyers at the publisher's. That's how I met Mosier. The publisher decided they wanted to change the contents of his book and Mosier was quite a stubborn old man, and he said there is no way I am going to let you do that. And they told him he was under contract and stuff and so they arranged a big meeting for him.

And Mosier was on his way to New York to meet with them and everybody was telling him he should get a lawyer and he stopped at Chicago, cause one of his students had told him a little bit about me and we had talked for about oh 25 hours and I looked over some of the agreements. I flew to New York with him. And I walked up and there was a table, a nice half round table with all of these lawyers sitting there. The next day when somebody asked them what happened, I believe the comment one of them made was, "I have no idea." He said, "I went to shake the guy's hand, the next thing I knew I was staring at my hand. And then there was a pen in it." I am going to teach you that technique, too. That one is designed for people that have fallen into a particular category called "Dick Heads." When they line up to manipulate somebody, suddenly you don't go into the subject matter, you go into an unconscious state, where they can not interfere unhealthfully. But the majority of what we are going to deal with has to do with the way people make decisions. If you know how people make decisions, and you know what information to get, and you know how they process information then whatever it is you are going to tell them, you can package perfectly enough, that it will go through that system so they can maximally understand it. It may not still be perfect.

I have a friend who is a very very good real estate agent and I was waiting for him in his office and he had some other guys who worked for him and somebody came in and said, "Do you have properties, in [a certain area] where the houses on that property have a huge back yard?" And the guy looked down and he goes, "Uh, well not right now." It's a very bad answer by the way, "not right now." And the person turned away and started to walk out the door and I said, "Excuse me." By the way, I wasn't a real estate agent and I didn't work there. We were meeting to have lunch, but it seemed like a rare and unprecedented opportunity to practice skills that I didn't have. And I said, "Let me ask you a question," I said, "What are you going to do with a big back yard?" And the woman turned around and said, "Well I have nine children?" And I said, "Oh, you have nine children and you really like to pay taxes." And she said, "Well I have nine children." (In the U.S. that means you don't pay a lot of taxes, by the way.) And I said, "Well, I didn't mean that kind of taxes, I mean property taxes." And she said, "I don't understand," I said, "Well the more land you have the more property taxes you pay." And then in the area they were talking about they charge by the inch. So I said to her, I said, "Let me see." And I turned to him and I said, "Do you have any properties that back up to a school?" and he said, "Oh, yeah." And I said, "Why don't you get a house and let the school mow the lawn and your children can play in it. Wouldn't that be easier or do you like mowing lawns? How old are your children? Old enough to do all the work and pay the taxes?" And she said, "Well gee I never thought of that." Now the difference is, when people tell you the result they want, a lot of times they tell you how to get it, not what the result is.

Now when I went down to my friend who had the Mercedes lot I said I need a new hobby, I said, "I have several other hobbies, but I need a new hobby, so what I'd like to do is come down a couple of days a week and sell cars." And he looked at me and he went, "What are you talking about?" And I said, "Well I built this model and I'd like to try it out." Now this was, by the way, in the middle of the oil embargo, this is when the only kind of car that you could sell was one that you could put in your pocket. Right, people were buying these little Toyota Corollas, little tiny things and that's when you went (nnnnn). It's not like they are now, where the big tough cars of those days, they were like you know the only thing was they got was a lot of gas mileage but that's because half the time you had your foot outside the door. And he told me, "You could come down here," he said, "but we didn't sell a car in the last three months," and he said, "I think you're wasting your time." And I said, "Oh, that's what makes it fun." Because every time I found a really professional engineer of influence, the one thing they've had as a solid belief is that challenge is exciting and that's where you get to learn new skills. It's not like, "Grrrrr, it's gonna be so haaard," or "But, I don't want to," "But it's too expensive." They start sounding like dental drills.

So I went in and there were these four other salesman, and they were depressed. They were sitting at their desks. I remember the first day I went in because one guy who had his face down and this other guy was chewing, he had a little piece of weed or something. I thought, boy they're out there prospecting their asses off, huh? So, I came in and I looked around and sure enough, they weren't popping in going, "Gee, can I have a Mercedes?" You know, because to begin with people are going, "the price of gas is going up, DA DA, DA DA." So I asked him, I said, "Well you guys, you're not really doing anything," I said, "Maybe you could answer a few questions," I said, "How many cars do we have here to sell today?" And they showed me the new cars and this is a small town so they didn't have a lot, and I said, "Is this it?" I mean they only had like twenty five cars and I had big plans. So this one guy looks at me and he says, "I hate you young guys," he says, "You think you can do anything," he says, "I've been a car salesman for thirty-five years and in the state of this economy and with the oil crisis and for every commercial we could even show they have news and everything saying you shouldn't buy a big gas guzzler," he said, "a Mercedes with a V8! What the hell makes you think you can sell one of these?" And I said, "Are you a bettin' man? Let's put something on this, something humiliating." Well I thought I might motivate them a little bit. So I said, "I'll tell you what. I bet you my pants, against your pants that I can sell more than one car by the end of the day, as long as someone can fill out the paper work, no one showed me how to do that, yet, and I have a phobia of it." I gave myself one and from out of this little window, a female voice went, "I'll fill it out for you, especially if I can see him with his pants off."

So I said, "Great!" I hopped into a 450 SLC Mercedes, top of the line at that time, going for $35,000 now it goes for I don't know a few zillion, I don't know what they go for. A beautiful silver gray, brand new, it had that smell of a new car. And I drove off the lot and drove away. Now, I came back about an hour and a half later with four people in the car and each of them bought a car. Two of them had to order it because we didn't have the cars. Alright, then I had the guy hand me his pants and he was sitting there in his boxer shorts, really depressed. These other people are in there filling out the forms and the lady's in there laughing her ass off every once in a while and she comes over and looks out the window and giggles. She knew that if those guys got out there and did something it couldn't be as bad as it was. One of the guys looks at me and he goes, "Where did you go?" and I went, "I went to the country club." And he went, "What?" And I said, "I went to the bar at the country club, there wasn't anybody here. And I just drove up, I opened all four doors, I walked inside and I turned around and I said, 'Can I have your attention everyone? Is there anybody who wants to feel wonderful for the rest of their life?'" I mean who is going to go, "Not me, I felt wonderful before. What I need is a good case of depression."

Pretty soon I had them out there smelling the leather, imagining what it would be like to "drive down the road and knowing that when you buy a car like this you can't be stupid enough to believe that the oil crisis will go on forever, but this thing has a great big tank, it's got guts, it has a huge tank in it. You may guzzle more gas, but you don't have to go as often. And you know for a few bucks, we can put a reserve tank in the trunk, too, if you want us to, and when you've had this car for a certain number of years you can trade it in and get even a better car, because it drops down in value a little bit but it comes back up, its' done it for centuries. Unless you like spending $12,000 on a car and then three years later having it be worth a dollar. Of course, there is that other thing too, which is, you know, when you drive up and your clients see you are successful and in a brand new car, they know your business is going better than theirs and perhaps you'll get more contracts. Of course you're not interested in such things as that. The question is, how good do you want to feel?"

Now there are a few other tricks I know that helped us along which I am going to teach you. But while they were doing this, I suddenly stopped and I went, "Excuse me, I forgot to ask you. Some of these people have cars. Do you take trade-ins?" The guy said, "Of course we take trade-ins. He said, "We've got so many trade-ins because you know what people trade in on a Mercedes? An old Cadillac, an old Lincoln Continental!" He said, "Behind that building over there is over a hundred Lincolns and Cadillacs, ranging from fifteen to twenty years." And I said, "Can we sell them?" And the guy said, "No, you can't sell them. Nobody will buy them." And I said, "But are we allowed to sell them?" And he said, "Yeah." And I said, "How much do they cost?" and the guy gave me a list and I looked at it and I went, "Wow!" and he looked at me and he said, "This is the middle of the oil crisis, you can't sell a Cadillac." And I said, "Excuse me" and I went right out the front door, across the street to the Toyota lot and stood on the side walk. You can't walk on the pavement but I can stand on the sidewalk. And the salesman walks up and he's got this guy with him and he starts showing him this car, and so I said to the guy who he was selling the car to, I said, "Excuse me mister. You don't have a family, do you?" and he said, "Well, yeah I do." And I said, "Well then you don't like them, very much." And he said, "Well I love my family." And I said, "Do you know what it takes to crush one of these cars? Imagine, you're gonna save a little gas and your son is in the back with his head smashed and his arms broken?" I said, "You are going to feel like a heel, man." And he goes well, "What can I do?" and I said, "Well you know what I'd do? What I'd do is realize that for a fourth of the price of this car, you can buy a used Lincoln, have $9000 left over to buy gas and parts and it will have leather seats and power windows and if you get hit by one of these you can scrape it off with a brillo pad."

I sold 120 cars in less than a month. I broke a record but it was used cars. It didn't amount to that much. Except I could double the price and still sell them. That's neat you know, the commission left on the Mercedes at that point of time was nothing compared to what I can make off of an old Cadillac. I sold everybody I knew one. I bought one. I bought one and drove it for years. It was great, I paid $2000 for a Lincoln Continental and I drove it for ten years. And I was hit four times. And each time, all it took was a brillo pad, because that big Lincoln bumper out there, you know, and that Toyota . . . actually one time I wasn't even in the car. I was parked and this guy came around the corner and BAP!!! hit the trunk. His car flipped on top of mine. Alright, when I came out they were just taking him away in the ambulance and I reached over and went (Flip) like this and the car spun and fell on the ground and the policeman said, "What the hell do you think you are doing?" and I said, "Well I was just getting the dust off my car so I could go home." That's a good selling point for a car when you can wipe other cars off of it.

Now, to me the major thing was, that my view point was that: what I was looking at, other people weren't looking at, at that moment in time. Now, they were trying to save a few bucks so the question is, for how long? Because when you change the length of time you think about things, you start to add other dimensions.

When people negotiate . . . As a matter of fact, I was used as an arbitrator several times. And most of the time I found that the problem wasn't that either side couldn't give up or couldn't give this. It's that neither side was asking for enough. Because when you expand what both sides asking for, it gives you a wider range to negotiate, as long as they understand what the end result is.

The National Association of Respiratory Therapists hired me because at one point in time there was a great schism in their community and I mean they were just going all out. These were the people that have breathing drug machines. It started out, doctors had some people and these machines take a long time to run so they taught these people to run them and pretty soon it became a whole field and they had junior college courses that went on for two years and you got a license. But, then there was another one that went on for one year that got a license and then there were all these people that learned from the doctors that didn't have a license, and they had a national organization and they were ripping it apart trying to decide what were they going to do. Should it be a two year program, should it be a four year program, should we cut off all the people that learned to do from practical skill, should we grandfather them? Oh my God, let's hate each other, and they attacked one another. Now, I went in the night before and I had them each write up a proposal for what it was that they wanted. And I changed one word. One word in both proposals and kind of shuffled them together because they pretty much said the same thing. The word is desirable. And I read it out loud and said, " Is there anybody here, that disagrees with this?" And nobody raised their hand. So before we even started, see usually it takes time to negotiate something, this took thirty-two minutes to read the thing and say "Hello" and ask the question and I said,

"So there is no conflict." They all looked at each other, here these people have been fighting for five years, they agreed with one another.

It sounds like marriage doesn't it. I always loved that, when I hear that, his wife turns around and says to her husband, "You're only trying to do that to make me feel good." You've all heard it too, haven't you? It's just that thing that when you get into a certain state, you don't have the flexibility to do the things that you want. So number one is having a road map, number two then becomes having a set of beliefs that may or may not be true. But, if you believe, you can sell to anyone. If you believe that challenge is fun, and if you believe all you have to do is vary your behavior in order to get the responses you want from other people you have the foundation, you have the same foundation as people who are closing at a 97% close ratio. All you have to do is learn to be a little bit outlandish.

Now the next thing is, is that all of these people had intrinsic sets of skills and knew *when* to use them.

What we have here is for you to use these things to engineer your influence and build your business in ways that would increase your earnings, your sales and your personal success and well being. We want you to triple your income in less than half the time and double that again. When you stop and consider that there was a time when there once was no money, and look around you now and see how much there is, that ought to be one reason to understand that you don't have to work as hard as you've been working to get better results.

More than anything else, this is an attitude. It's a way of life. The most successful people are those people who truly "believe" in what they do. Not that they just say they do. They have a passion for what they do. They wouldn't trade their careers or professions for anything else. They turn down get rich quick schemes. They focus on their own goals and they have the competence as well as the confidence to achieve what they want. Their attitude keeps them healthy, hungry and moving in the direction that has them achieve their own desires effortlessly. They believe in what they are doing. They are congruent in what they say and how they behave in support of what they say.

You have to be congruent.

☙ CHAPTER TWO:
THE SELLING PROCESS

When you look at the selling process, we like to start from the end. Many sales training programs start with the beginning of the process. After all, when you know where you're going, it's much easier to get there. Then you run the process backwards for yourself so you know what steps you take to get there. And the steps are general enough to give you the flexibility to make the changes you'll need to make for each situation.

Take this for example. No matter what you thought you sold, you sell feelings. Period. Those feelings are *trance-lated* by your customers. And each one of them will do it differently. This you can take to the bank. So you first want to find out what the feeling is they want and how they interpret this with their language, both verbal and nonverbal. Then, you take them there.

There is this one case that we stumbled upon accidentally. There was this couple who was buying a new home. He was being transferred by his company and she had to relocate with him. This is a very common situation. We are also seeing the opposite.

Now the saleswoman was about to show the couple the home. They already met and went over the particulars. But she also knew of the wife's reluctance to move anywhere. Now this is what I call "lucky." As they approached the home, they walked up the front walkway. She opened the first door and the wife says, "Wait!" This is where the salesperson usually says to themselves, "Oh, No. Now what?" But the wife says, "Open that door again." The saleswoman did the smartest thing she could have done at that moment. She closed the door and opened it! Imagine that! She didn't ask why; she didn't ask what for. She closed the door and opened it again. The wife looks at her husband and says, "It squeaks just like our door at home." The saleswoman started making excuses when the client said, "I already feel at home here. Let's buy this one." This is the greatest, and almost shortest sale of this magnitude that I know of. This is a great example of how simple the sale is sometimes. The saleswoman probably would not have elicited this information from the customer, but the information also was probably there somewhere during the interview. We don't really know. But the fact is, that the sound of the front door opening *made her feel at home.* Any professional salesperson on the planet has to go "Wow!" I call this *"very lucky!"* Of course, I consider luck to be the combination of fine skills and the ability to recognize opportunity when it's knocking and do something with it.

Now the selling process includes some of your own content. That's the specific context related material of your business. If you sell cars, be able to provide congruent information about the car. It does help to know the horsepower, etc.

Now the process begins with rapport. This subject is still over taught. The essence of rapport is that it is a state of mind that begins with kinesthetics. Sure, you can body match, match breathing and all that. You don't have to spend three days body matching to get rapport. You pace then lead. Pace, pace pace, pace, pace, pace pace just isn't going to do it. Remember the objective is to be able to influence the situation. Keep that in mind. When people teach pacing for three, even four days, it says something about the ability of the person to notice what's going on around them. I mean, what does it take to look at the customer and match their posture? It requires a simple, yet, somewhat seemingly elusive skill. It's basic. It's simple. It's: open your eyes and your ears and all your senses and notice what's going on around you. Your customer, or your client, has all the information you need to help them. They will give it to you. You don't have to go inside your head to figure out what's going on. If you do, you just made the second fatal mistake of any professional communicator. Not only will they tell you and show you what's going on inside their head, they'll even give you the solution opportunities they need. If you know where you're going, and you know what's there, you'll know what's missing. If you go inside your own head, you'll miss something outside. And believe me, there's a lot to miss if you're not there at the party.

So the process of rapport is important but we're not going to spend a lot of time on it. Any matching you do needs to be tested ASAP and regularly. Like driving your car. You drive down the highway. You make sure it's between the lines. Then what, you go to sleep? I don't think so. You make sure you keep it between the lines. And you adjust. Constantly. The most important thing to remember is that if rapport gets broken you reestablish it – quickly – whatever it takes. The best way to keep rapport going is that you must *demonstrate* understanding. Let me repeat that – *DEMONSTRATE UNDERSTANDING.* That means behaviorally. Saying, "I understand" isn't enough and it can even sometimes work against you because it could be insulting to the customer. *Demonstrate understanding behaviorally.* (mirror)

I like to tell people that because salespeople already have a lot to overcome, and much of it is undeserved in many places. It's like consultants. Many people think and say that consultants are the people who come into your company and tell you what you already know and charge you for it. Well, that's not necessarily true, although we have seen it in many cases.

I had a guy call me one day to ask me to pitch him for a seminar we were conducting the following day. He didn't outright ask that way. He called and asked, "Is this the place that's conducting the seminar tomorrow?" I, of course said, "Yes." He then said, "Well, why should I come to your seminar?" I had a number of choices at this point in time and decided to conduct another of my experiments. I said, "You shouldn't." I wanted to again test the generalization that most people don't do their shoulds but they do their shouldn'ts. He responded, "Then why not?" Then I told him that he would show up, join the seminar, learn lots of great things, use them, watch his life turn in the right direction and be more successful than he's ever been. He goes, "Fine! Then I'll see you tomorrow." And he did.

Sales people don't have the right to sell something just because they're there. You earn the right to influence someone. You can earn it quickly and precisely. Just like the therapy business, your customers pay you to help them get what they want so they can feel good. They don't pay for you to feel good. You get to do that anyway.

So, you earn the right to influence. Then you move on in the process and keep it going.

The most successful salespeople that we know store their selling experiences, both successful and otherwise, in such a way that what you do is set up resource files in your mind because all experience is useful in some given context. What works today may not work tomorrow and what didn't work today may work tomorrow. You never know what may work. Remember, your customer will always communicate what's going on and what the solution opportunities are. You may be surprised at what works and when.

Another of the important things you can learn about the selling process isn't only to make the right choice at the choice point, but when, to make it, especially since time and space are relative.

When you do the exercises, that we provide, to build more behavioral flexibility into your communicating process, you begin to reinforce your understanding of language processing and using it more fully. We find that most people who need more options in their lives also need more flexibility in their language and voice qualities as well. You can call it what you want, if you can't say it well, you can't do it well. Build on top of that the auditory qualities of a champion and Zing! you've got your winning combination!

❧ CHAPTER THREE:
THE BASIC STUFF

We're going to touch on what some of the basics are for those of you who are novices to NLP. For those of you who consider yourselves to be veterans in the field, you may, of course skip this section, but then you'll never know what you missed because the ways I've learned what I've learned is to continue to be unreasonably curious about what others are doing in business, in sales, in marketing, especially the most successful people out there.

So there are skills for example, in NLP they teach you about pacing. And things like, you know, you can breathe at the same rate as someone, you can speak at the same rate they speak. If you have somebody who thinks primarily in visual images, you can describe things to them in visual images. But you see there is a time and a place to use that. And there are times and places not to; and knowing which are which is based on your ability to see and hear things on the outside.

What makes the difference in the rapport process is understanding the directions people move in. Since a decision is a nominalization, it is relatively stationary. Turning this event into a process, we need to consider whether or not it will move towards being executed, or will it be "put aside." That's most of the problem with decision making. Many decisions are made and are lackluster to being executed. Listening to the sentence structure of the whole representation of the process will help you understand whether or not the decision will be executed. Remember, one of the more important things in the choice point is *when*.

How and when people move in directions and in which direction is very useful information. Now let's back up a little. One of the reasons why we point this direction thing out is because of the way people will respond to different stimuli. The towards and away-from sorting pattern is one to learn about and so is how to use it in a three dimensional model. Now, run through this the element that the brain likes what's the same, and learns by noticing what's different, it's what I like to call the "push-pull" element.

We teach you, for example, that speaking to a rhythm will tend to build a rhythm for the listener. As choice points for the communicators, when you interrupt the rhythm momentarily you open the opportunity to embed another structure, then slide back into the rhythm again. This particular demonstration of rapport through sameness is the one we want you to understand here. Sure, body matching is a neat visual demonstration, but it's not necessarily the most useful. Because there are so many people who have learned about this by now it sort of turns into the old "who's matching who game." We don't recommend this for success.

I remember once where I met with these three managers from the same company. We were going in to sell them our services. They all had done their research on NLP (or what they thought was NLP) and "had all the answers" about what the consultant should be able to do. One of them even tipped his hat when he told me that they had interviewed another consultant who "did" NLP and didn't walk his talk. He didn't even bother to demonstrate to them that he understood what they wanted. They told this guy what they wanted and he told them that it wasn't. That he had even better stuff than that.

So I meet with these three guys. When we first met, I looked at the first one, a young guy with very expensive clothes, Italian silk suit and tie and really expensive boots. I walked up to him, introduced myself and said, "Wow, Bill. Great suit. Italian silk, isn't it?" He smiled, looked at his suit and said, "Yeah, thanks!" He was easy, but I wanted to get one in the bank early. I met the others and we went into their meeting room. I noticed that one of them, the prime decision maker, by the way, appeared to me to be going out of his way to mismatch my body posture. He was really creative, too. So I asked him a question about the training he wanted and he spoke for about a minute, or so. I then looked at the others and spoke to them. I used his voice tone, tempo, rhythm, inflections, etc. while speaking to them. I didn't even bother to look at him. After a few minutes I did the obligatory rapport check, I touched my cheek, and I saw him touch his out in my peripheral vision. I paused, turned my head and smiled. He laughed and said, "Wow, how did you do that?" I told him we teach it in the sales program. He laughed and asked again. Interestingly enough, he appreciated the idea that I could be as tenacious as he could, he gave us the contract. Interesting match, I'd say. You see, the communication processes that do occur can be redirected easily. We tend to learn through difference, even though we tend to like what's the same. *Get their attention first.* Without it, they're wasting your time.

When you talk to somebody, where you stand, how you move, the tone you use, every nuance of communication becomes vital, because it influences a particular process. And it's the process by which people make the decision whether or not to buy something. Or whether or not to change a belief about something. Because some people sell ideas, like those people that come to your house on Sunday morning, or worse on Saturday morning. The ones that come by with the comic books, they scare me, people like that, because they come by and they go, "Have you accepted Jesus as your personal savior?" And I go, "No, not today." They go, "Why not?" and I go, "Because I'm Jewish. And we are still waiting. We are sure there is a Messiah coming, we just don't think it was him. But it's okay if you want to think it's him, as long as you don't think it's him on my doorstep at six in the morning." Then I found one of the ways of convincing them to leave is to take your clothes off.

After all, think about it, some people get confused because when they build convictions or beliefs they build them so that if any other ideas are around it they can't detect it. They simply delete it. Now this is what happens when people come in, because I have people that come in and they said to me, "Well you know, I want to buy a station wagon." At that time Mercedes didn't make a station wagon. And I look at him, and I go, "No you don't." And they go, "Yeah, yeah I have to have a station wagon." And I go, "No you don't." Now, that's not pacing is it? See these NLP people get really stuck on it. It goes pace, pace lead lead lead. It's not pace pace pace pace pace pace pace pace get frustrated, to self criticism.

The representational systems are the first choice of successful communicators. Actually paying attention to anything in the process is a good start One of the easiest ways to begin influence is to pay attention to the representational systems of the customer. They can change with context so, once you have their attention, pay attention to what they are doing while they're saying what.

I have some friends who own a stereo business and while I was in there one day they asked me if I could give them some selling ideas. They were working on my car and so I said, "Sure." They had a guy who really knows his stuff technically but it seemed that he couldn't get enough sales. He was a really nice guy . . . but . . . they weren't paying him to be a nice guy, they were paying to get results.

Well, I went into the selling area and he really did know his stereos and sound systems. He could rattle off specifications and all kinds of things for the customers and they weren't listening to him. They would come in and say, "I want to *look* at some stereos." This guy would respond by saying something like "Well, this one here has really good sound, blah blah blah hear it blah blah blah, etc." Pretty simple. The customers would even say things like "This *looks* like it sounds really good." I don't know about you but this seems like an opening opportunity to me. A lot of these people were basing their primary decision criteria on *how it looks*! They want blinking lights, brushed chrome on black panels and lots of neat-looking dials. Imagine that stereo companies even built "graphic equalizers" so people could *see what it sounds like*! Take these cues as they are presented. I even have some friends who have said to me, "Hey, have you *seen* my new stereo? Let me *show* it to you." This guy has seen the benefits is now selling stereos like there's no tomorrow.

Track the sequence of the rep systems from the beginning. We receive information in all the senses: we see, hear, feel, smell, and taste. We process the information, we store it, we retrieve it, we reprocess it: we see it, hear it, feel it, smell it, taste it, or some combination of these; then rerepresent it and then communicate it. Do you see what I'm saying? Getting a handle on it? Grasping it? Can you feel what I'm saying? Because that is the way that people will communicate. And, of course, there are unspecified words like manage, decide, know, etc.

So, what happens is, many people get caught up in their own learned patterns. They may go, "See this, see that", visual, visual, visual. The other person person is saying, "Talk to me. Talk to me. Tell me more." And then we want to show them things? They don't want to be shown things. They want to hear about them. It's a mismatch in communication. Now, because you have choices in your communication you can communicate the same idea in all rep systems. It's very possible to do that. Does this look interesting? Does it sound like something you would like to pursue further? Perhaps get a little bit more of a handle on it? Can you see how subtleties like this can have you enjoy the sweet smell of success? Again, these are very basic skills.

Pay attention to how the other person communicates because that's how they communicate. People will ask us how do they know what rep system the other person is using. Our reply: "Open your eyes and ears and all your senses and pay attention to what's going on."

Just paying attention will get you a lot of information. Most people really know what they want when they want it. They may not know how to get it in the best way. The selling process is only one of two things: either they pretty much know what they want, or they don't. When they do know, you give it to them. When they don't, you teach them how to buy it.

You'll remember about eye accessing cues. This was a really great discovery since it went unnoticed for years. Well, it's still good information about where someone's eyes move when they're accessing information and validating the congruence of their communication but it's not nearly as valuable as noticing where they move their eyes to after they have the information.

For example, think about something that you believe without a doubt. Like, do believe that's it's important to breath? Now where did your eyes move to in order to *retrieve* the information? And now where *is* the information? In front of you and down right or higher, for example? Ask this question of others and notice what you get as a response. Notice if they first remember the information (eye access up and left, for example), then *where do they place the picture?* This is very valuable information. Of course, it does require that you see it first. When you see it, you can use it.

Resourcefulness is a valuable choice for life. So, to begin with, there're some things you need to do with yourself first. I mean, if you wake up in the morning and go, "Oh, no, not another day at work (grrr)", that's not going to work real well. Get started right.

Because the other foundation that we are going to have to build in this area is that nothing of what we will teach you will work if you don't internally make of yourself something which is more powerful. And I mean more powerful than you were the day before. You need to start each day by making yourself more powerful, more motivated. I wake up in the morning and I open the drapes and look at all the buildings full of money out there. And I say to myself, "Ahhh, I want it." I look at the telephone . . . you know some people who did telemarketing have phobias about cold calling. Not a good combo. And I ask them, "How many calls do you make a day?" And they all go, "Well, I don't know, six." And I go, "Six? You know, I make six before I get out of bed." And I don't even have anything to cold call about. I just do that to practice. I call up and go, "Do you like diamonds?" And they go, "Who is this?" And I go, "It's not important. Just wanted to know if you like big diamonds." And they go, "Are you one of my relatives?" And I go, "No, I just wanted to know if you like big diamonds." And they go, "Yeah" and I go, "Is your husband around?" And they go, "Yeah." And I go, "How would you like to be able to get him to want to buy you a big a diamond?" And they go, "Well, I don't think I can get him to do that." And I said, "I don't think you could either . . . without my help, of course. But you do deserve it, don't you?"

Wouldn't it be something that would be there for the rest of your life? Wouldn't it be nice to have something that you could look at everyday that made your soul reverberate with pleasure? You see, your ability to change your tonality and your belief system and to have fun . . . what a great profession.

Now, let me ask you to do the following thing because the answer to what we want to learn is, of all places, inside your head. Because we, as sales people, are the most powerful consumers of all. We can't help ourselves. We order out of catalogs, from television. We love sales because we love buying. Own up to it. We are the best ones of all. As soon as we get a buck in our pocket, we are out there looking at whatever trinket we can find. We are like pro's. If it shines, we'll look at it. And then we'll consider, "Maybe we can sell that, too." That's why some of us float from selling one thing to another to another, we just like the activity. When you do it well, isn't it as good as sex? Well, almost.

Hey when I was single, I met a lot of people selling Mercedes and old Cadillacs. Sometimes now, I just walk in the store and sell things even if I don't work there. Just for the hell of it. I wonder, I ask myself, "Can I sell that stuff?" And I look at that exercise equipment and I think, "God, it amazes me, people actually buy this stuff. I got to go in, and see how do you sell this stuff?" And the next thing I know I have exercise equipment all through my house. I am very convincing.

Now, Let me ask you to do the following, I want you to think of an example of each of these things. First one and then the other. First, I want you to think of something where you walked in, you looked at it, you absolutely had to have it, you bought it and you're delighted with it? Okay. Then, after you think about that, then I want you to stop . . . and I want you to think about something where you went in and you knew you wanted it, and you knew it was the perfect thing and you didn't buy it.

Okay, now when you do this, I want you to look at one in your mind . . . now look at the other. I'm going to ask you the question: Are the pictures in the same place in your mind? Physically located? I am going to ask you are they the same size? Are they both color or black and white or is there a difference: is one a movie and one a slide or are they both slides or both movies? Is the sound the same? Is the size of the images the same? Or as you go back and forth in your mind is there a lot of differences between these two things?

DEMONSTRATION

Okay, Peter, I see your nodding. Is there a difference? They are both in the same place? Just start at the beginning here, Peter, we'll inch our way along. Okay, now, if you guys could watch, come up here, Peter, you've got to come up here, they've got to see this, this is too good. Now, the stuff that we told you about accessing cues, some of you know about and some of you haven't. Let me just run you through this. When people make pictures in their mind, when people make images, they have a tendency, first to have to get the image, they have to move their eyes to get the image and then they look at where it is. So you know, when, for example Peter, what was the first one, what did you buy? "A tape recorder." A tape recorder. Okay, I got it. And the thing that you didn't buy, what was that? "A car." It was a car. Now, can you guys see these images are not in the same place? The image of the tape recorder is on the right and image of the car is on the left.

Now let me tell you something. This is a big thing that sales people do, which manages to decrease their income profoundly (for those of you who want to get poor.) They have a tendency to walk around in these images. They get in peoples' faces, and talk to them and they can't see a thing. Cause remember, we know there are some differences, we know that number one, we don't want images over here (gesturing over to the left) do we? We want them over there (gesturing to the right) don't we? Cause that's where he buys them. We also know, as he said, that there is a certain intensity of color. Which one is closer, by the way? Big surprise! (as he points to the one he bought). Now did he just show us how much closer? Thank you Peter. Now, when you think about this car and you didn't buy it, that's because it wasn't the "right" thing, you know. That's right.

Now let's take this image of the car, just for the sake of things. What I want you to do is bring it around over here (to where the tape recorder image is) and move it up and change the intensity of the color. (Richard anchors the response) That was subtle. I like the way . . . "damn he anchored him on the shoulder, see that hand up there?" We do recommend that you do notice these things. But we recommend you're slightly more subtle than that. Do you see what I am saying?

So anyway, I have this old Cadillac, Peter. And I just want you to take a look at it. It's just a 1974 Cadillac but, see what I mean vrrm. There's no car and he's ready to buy it. Look at his face: he's thrilled. And the only thing is that it has a jet engine on it. Well, Richard likes to go very, very, very fast. That way, when I am chased by the police I can out run them. Then wings pop out the side, and you take off. So, they watch you sail away and they go, what was that? Right, and then you have a loud speaker out of the back: "UFO." That's what I am going to sell next year is UFO's. Hum, want to go for a ride on a UFO? Peter, don't you think it would be useful, don't you? Wow. Wow, that would be great! All you have to do is invest a little right now. Yeah yeah. Thank you Peter, you can sit down. *(End of demonstration)*.

Now. The other piece in this. One piece has to do with knowing how people make decisions in their mind and being able to make it work within those things. The last piece we are going to work with here, is that all of you need to learn to increase your own enthusiasm. One of the things about selling and negotiating, in fact, one of the things about life is that, if you don't make things more exciting, they get duller. This is true about people, it's true about things, it's true about everything. You need to be able to create an internal state which makes the activity itself wonderful. You need, for example, to be able to move through the world with no fear. Only excitement!! You need to look at the activity the way you would a great meal. See I know people who look at the people who come in and they go in and they go, "Oh, shit." And they come up and they go, "Can I help you?" (muffled) People go, "Get away from me!" You need to be able to walk up to that person and say, "Excuse me, sir, but you are in the wrong aisle." And they say, "How do you know that?" "Because these are not worthy of you. This stuff is junk. You look like somebody who wants to have quality in their life." Who's gonna say, "Not me, I want garbage in my life"? I'll tell you about this rhetorical question thing, because one of the things that you want to do, is always remember the entire communication, you want to keep people in the state of answering, yes. Constantly. You want them to feel yes, in every fiber of their soul. The other thing that you want to do is to make sure that the activity is enjoyable, because you have to create a great internal state in yourself so that you can create one in them. Because you need to create a state that's dynamic, that feels better than anything else. Because it's not that people couldn't buy products through the mail, that you could just send everybody catalogs and they could just look it up. You know, they are trying this over the telephone, now everybody has their modem, and is going to go shopping. You know what? They have

to still put sales people at the other end. Even if they are simu-
lated ones.

Without salespeople you cannot induce the response that it
takes to attach to a product to make it powerful enough that you
can get people to respond. Because the important thing that you
sell with every product or every service is that every time they
look at it or think about it they should feel good. No matter what.
This is what you do for a living. You make sure that decisions are
permanent, that decisions make them feel good and the other
thing that I require is that they bring twenty clients within the
next six months. Or feel bad. Actually, I make it so that they want
to come back so much, that they are always dragging people over.
I make is so that they have an intense feeling inside of them, that
makes them want to do that. Cause I think it's part of what you
get, it's part of your commission, is that you spend a lot less time
prospecting.

Now, there are different kinds of engineering. Some of you are
probably managers, in which case you don't have to get them to
bring you new people. They are there already. But there are parts
of this process that are going to apply to all of you. And I want to
start by having you do something which is the most important
thing of all, which is begin to turn your own internal state on as
an asset so that when you get up in the morning and when you
get in your car and you drive, and when you walk in there, (I don't
care what state you want to be in on the way there), when you
walk in the door, you should light up like a bulb. Now, if you are
smart, when the sun comes through your eyelids . . . That's the
way I like to do it because I like to launch into my day. The idea
of waking up and going "I don't want to get up." just doesn't
strike me as a good idea.

It seems like a waste of time to have to wait until you have to
urinate to get up. It seems to be the primary motivator on the

planet right now. People wake up and go, "I don't want to get up, if you don't get up, you'll be late (Bmmmf)." Painting pictures of being late, feeling depressed and stuff. They go through this nonsense and suddenly they have to pee so they get up. This doesn't strike me as the best internal strategy. And probably the reason things aren't as dynamic as they could be is because your own internal states aren't as dynamic. So we are going to start out with a little exercise. Exercise number one will give you not only some more of the internal states that I think are really congruent with having more flexibility, but it is also going to give you something else. I want you to learn to watch the changes in peoples' faces, as you induce them.

Now, those of you who have had NLP training before . . . forget it.

We don't do it that way. This way I don't want anybody squinting to see responses. See, they do this NLP, I heard, and people do this stuff: "Remember a time when you were real excited." They look and they look for minimal changes in lips and stuff. Bullshit, okay? We are looking for ones where the whole person just lights up like a neon light! If you don't see that, than you have to *change your behavior*. The trick is you need to learn to be congruent. That's when words and behavior match at the same moment in time. When you ask somebody to think of a time, you need to exude it. You can't go, "Well think of a time you were real thrilled" And do it with a whiny voice tone. And I know when you do this exercise I'm going to hear it. And when you feel the hand hit you on the side of the head you will know why. I've discovered if I hit them just hard enough the ideas will go in.

Now we are going to start with kinesthetic anchoring. But we are going to move onto other kinds, because you can anchor in different ways, sometimes you touch people sometimes you don't. You see, the funny thing is I noticed that therapists and people in the field of psychology only touch someone else only when they first meet and when they are leaving. But when you walk into offices, stores, or hardware stores there is always a guy who has his hands on somebody from behind showing him something. So don't tell me you don't touch people. Cause I know you do. It's just that you do it without knowing about it. The trick is to do it at the right time. And what we want to concentrate on here is to begin to build some powerful states, so I want to show you a different kind of anchoring. Alright now, what we are going to do is we are going to make anchors, but the anchor we are going to make is one which is called a sliding anchor, what we are going to do is keep inducing more and more states in anchoring something by distance. In other words, we are going to make a little mark and then we are going to start at the beginning and go a little further and then go a little bit further. You can do this with your hand in the air or you can do this on people's skin. But you must be very precise at the moment you do it or you can get all kinds of things that you wouldn't know you get. I've had people say to me, "Well, I am just sure I don't want to buy a Mercedes." And I say, "Are you sure enough to be unsure?" And they say, "Yeah." And I say, "Well then let's talk about it." Come with me. Okay, thank you very much.

Now, I'll tell you what I want you to do, I want you to find somebody out there that you don't know, it will be easier for you, cause the people that you already know, you've already got a lot of anchors with. I also want to make sure that you all have the ability to walk up to strangers. If any of you find difficulty in doing that it's because you're inside your head saying stupid things, like (mumble and yah mrbr, well I jajajjaja) Just shut up!

I don't want anybody talking to themselves behind the other's head unless they are saying things like "OOOOOOOOO," and if you start to say that other stuff, go "Shut up!" and say

"OOOOOOOOOO" and say it louder and then go "Ahhhhhhhhh". Otherwise somebody will be there first. And you know what, if you are always the second person to get the chance to sell something to somebody, and they always buy it from the first one then you won't sell anything. In fact, you won't have anything except regret. And then you will have to go to therapy for the rest of your life. It's really not worth it so when it's time just get up and walk over to someone. It will propel you forwards. Now when you get there, what I want you to do is to build a powerful internal state.

Now there is a little chart in the back of this book about anchoring that does it intellectually, but I want you to see what it looks like with someone.

Sit down with someone and ask them to just close their eyes for a minute. Now say to them "I want you to remember a time where you were excited" . . . or "a time where you were depressed" . . . or "a time where you felt angry" . . . or "a time where you felt invincible" . . . or whatever it is. And let them remember it. And I want you to see if you can notice any changes on their face. Now when those things exude to the point where they are maximally expressed, at that point in time, I am going to make a little anchor. Touch them, or make a sound, a gesture, or word.

Now you have them think about something else. " I want you to think about what you had for dinner last night." Notice the difference. You see, how does it feel that psychology missed this, that's what I want to know, a rock and roll musician finds this stuff. That's what I was doing at the time, I was playing the blues, you know. And I would ask audiences I'd go, "Are you guys feeling good?" And they would go, "Yeah!"

Now, go back and fire off the anchor for the person. Notice the response come back. Now this is my basic sales program: Induce good feeling; attach it to product. Or very importantly, you can also induce it and attach it to yourself, because you are a part of this, especially if it is a service, because *you, like me* want the best for yourself. *You, like me* want the best for yourself. Now this is a language pattern and we are going to get into those. They're fun.

You need to have a state which has got motivation, you've got to think of a time where you moved without hesitation. So what I want you to do is to ask that person to find a time like that, something like when they looked down there was a hundred dollar bill on the ground, right? Do you go, "Um don't touch that, you don't know where it's been". Not likely! (Vttttt) Down you go and you pick it up.

There are many other experiences where you move without hesitation. Now, you also want to find one where you felt somewhat flirtatious because you always need to be able to when you are doing sales or negotiating to be able to chide people from their positions. You don't want to flirt with them and kiss them and that kind of stuff. But one where you can just tease just enough and not too much so that you can maneuver people around. Go back to around when you were a teenager, you'll find a lot of this stuff. Find a time when you were able to induce that state that makes people feel a little giddy. Now, you want to find and for some of you, I know this is going to be the tough one, a time where you really had a good sense of humor. Okay, we're not talking lamp shades on the head here. We're talking about when somebody said something and something funny just pops into your head because it is the part that allows you to see the world differently. It adds flexibility. Then you want to find the time in your life where you have had the biggest, most intense and ferocious state of all. The time where you did something that not even you thought you would do. And it was fun.

Now for each of these, what I want you to do with a partner

is, I want you to have them think about it, see what they saw at the time, hear what they heard, and I want you to *be convincing*. Think of the time where you saw something and you knew you had to have it, and there was not a bit of hesitation at all. Build it up and as you build it up tell them to close their eyes, see what they saw at the time, hear what they heard and as you see the changes come up in their face I want you to mark it. Alright, now, then I want you to induce the second state the same way, start at the beginning, and layer it right over the top of the first one. What you are going to make for them is an anchor where they can reach it. To hell with this knee stuff they used to use. Put it somewhere where they can reach, put it down on their arm or shoulder, so that, if they reach over and fire off the anchor you are going to have all these things come pouring in at one time. Make the anchor, test the anchor, go to the next state, put it right over the top of the previous one when you get it, and you'll get both. At the third one, do this, so that internally you begin to build something and literally tell them when you fire it off. Make that picture in their head bigger, make it brighter, bring it up closer, have some real enthusiasm in your voice you know, where it was *REALLY INTENSE!*

Remember *congruency is everything in our business*. Remember the degree to which you can become more congruent in the way you do things is the degree to which your wealth increases directly. Think about it, if you could increase your close ratio by 300%, what do you think would happen to your life? "Oh, I'd have too much money and I would screw it all up and I would end up becoming an alcoholic, a drug addict, and end up buying a fancy sports car and killing myself. I'd just assume stay poor, thank you very much." That's not why you are learning this. You are learning this because you want more, because this isn't just about selling products, this is about engineering influence, about a lot of things, this is about getting a raise, this is about closing contracts. This is about starting your own businesses and I make that plural because I think now a days everybody must have more than one business.

An idea came to me as I was driving down the coast of Kona, and there it was: Mortuary and Donut Shop. And I thought, there is a guy with flexibility of behavior, right in the same building. Hey, if they could put those together, I figure you can put anything together. You know you should be able have all kinds of things. A place where you go in and buy software and underwear. Works for me. Some people need both. I go downtown to buy software and then I go, "Well, gee, you know, I wish there was a place close by where I could get underwear." I would have gone into an underwear store but there's no software there.

People tell me, "Well you know, we don't deal in that product." Do you realize that's like saying "I don't want that money." And I hear this constantly, I go in stores, I say, "Do you guys have video tape machines?" and he goes, "No we don't sell those", while he sweeps his hand across in front of him. They always make that gesture. No, no, no, not interested in that money. To me, I would go, "Just wait here." I'd look in the yellow pages and ask if I sell one of these can I have 20%. You know, it would only take a minute. "Oh no, you're not allowed to do that, excuse me, we don't sell those here. It's not in our nature, we are genetically immune from making this money." Uh mm.

See I'm willing to farm out anything. I'll be sitting in a store sometimes and people walk up to me, I don't know maybe it's just the way I look or something and that's because I watch them. They'll walk up and they'll say, "Excuse me, I'm really interested in this suit". And I go, "Wait here a minute." And I go to the manager, "If I sell this $2000 suit, before I pick mine up can I have 20%?" And if they say no I say to the customer, "Get out!" They'll never tell me that again. I go, "How about this next guy coming through the door? This could be a really bad day for you." Hey, what if it takes three hours for them to finish my suit? Hmmmm Hmmmmm.

Actually, there is a nice thing in San Francisco, this double business thing. There at the place where I get my suits they put a lunch counter in the middle of it. They serve fancy Italian food and it's just smack in the middle of this clothing store for no reason, no explanation, no nothing and you know, it's nice because when you are waiting for things you can go in.

But sometimes, you find yourself going in for a $10 lunch and coming out with a $2000 suit. And you ask yourself, "Well, I didn't know that I was that hungry." But you are sitting there and you pick up that menu and you go, "Yeah, that's what I want." And you order it and there's the suit. Ummm. Not a bad idea if you can get it in the right place. We could actually take a picture of them with a computer, generate an image, and hand it to him and he would be putty in our hands.

So to build up your attitude. Go find someone and do this.

We get a couple of interesting questions as we do seminars around the world. We ask them, "Did you make the pictures in your head and make them bigger and make them stronger and access the memories?" And they say, "No". It's like anything else. If you don't do things in your head to make your world more dynamic, it won't be. It's like I always tell people, if you are looking for what works, you'll find it and if you are looking for what will go wrong you will find it, too. If the way that you organize the world says that when people ask you to do things you don't do them, the name of that is "just stubborn." And if you want to be stubborn about making your life better, that is fine with me. In fact, if you need help making it worse, I know how to do that, too.

You know, go inside access bad feelings, amplify them, loop

them around, you know, and say to yourself, "Life is the pits, life is the pits, life is the pits." And it will be.

I am going to want you to go back and we've got one more piece of work we want to try here so that we can begin to open up the doorway.

See, I decided, unlike most people who like to chunk real small and spoon feed people, I like to chunk in great big pieces. I like to get the big pieces and then I figure you can always clean up the little ones. You guys can get a tape and learn language patterns and spend a little time doing that. We'll even cover some of these later in the book for you.

But if you can get the great big things about how the brain processes information and about how decisions go on, then you're much better. Whether it's a multimillion dollar contract or a can opener, the process itself is very very much the same. I mean there has to be certain things, certain pieces of information to get so that in your mind you move around the pictures you want in a certain way. Because I know that when I am buying something, it's very easy.

Consider the following line from one of the largest stereo chains in the world. And I walked in already wanting to buy something. I knew exactly what I wanted and in one store the guy convinced me not to buy it. I walked up and I looked at it and I pointed to a digital auditory tape machine and I said, "I want that." Now, I don't know about you guys, but that's where I figured you don't need to get their attention. You've already got that, you don't need any rapport at all. And you don't need any presentation. Right? Not unless you really want to screw things up. All you need to do is go, "Yes, sir." It seems like you are done. But this person looked at me and they said, "Well today, let me be honest with you." Something inside of me went, "Uh oh! That means that he's been lying to me all along." That one thing, one semantically dense utterance and I turned around and I said, "I am going to get out of here." And he said, "What's wrong?" And I said, "You!" I said, "I just wanted to buy it. I didn't want to be lied to."

We did an experiment in this furniture store in California. It's a big chain. They own furniture stores all over the place and I had some success in the furniture business teaching salesmen. We did an experiment, one day of training. And they have two stores, they had one on one side of the freeway and one on the other side of the freeway. We went in and trained the guys from one side of the freeway for one day. And for the next month they increased their close ratio between 10 and 50%. Just one day of training, by teaching them to do things like enjoy their work. One of the things that one of those guys in that store that we did the training in raised his hand and he said, "Look, sure you could, maybe you could vary your behavior for some people, but you know some of these people come in here, they bring somebody who's some kind of an expert, right? And if that person doesn't like what you have, there is nothing you can do to sell that person a piece of furniture." And I said, "Gee, it's funny when I hear that, I'm thinking of selling two pieces of furniture. Because if you get the right strategy from that person, if you pay enough attention to them you're going to be able to influence them." Now, inside the back of this book there is a page and it has a list of submodalities and then it says experience one and experience two. Now, I want you to try something like I demonstrated with Peter (earlier).

Now keep in mind the following things, also. People understand words at the same rate that they speak them. Now I'll tell you this is a lesson that was learned very hard for me. I had to go through a very painful experience, but there's a group of people involved in an activity called head hunting. This is where you go in and steal employees for fun and profit. And I was training a group of people and the way we did the training is we actually had the room set up with telephones all around the wall. And people would go out and they would call somebody and then they would come back and if they didn't get through and get what they wanted we would play a tape of it out loud and we would go through it. Well there was one guy who came back in and he played the tape. This prospect designed a certain kind of floppy disk something or other. I didn't understand technically what he did, but I understood this guy could talk slower than any human I have ever met on the face of the earth. Now, the guy told me, he had been trying to land this prospect for over two years because there were very few individuals who could do what he could do. And he couldn't understand it, he was offering him more money, he was offering him more job security. He said, "I tried offering him anything." But he wouldn't even meet with him. Now the thing is, this was the top guy at this company. Now this guy was good, he was snappy, he was quick, he was bright, but when he called this prospect up, this prospect spoke very, very slowly,

"Helllooo, thiiissss iiiissss Geeooooorrrrggggge SSSchhwwaaaarrrrrttttttsssss, HHHHowwww mmmmmaaaaayyyyy IIIIIII hhhhhellllllpppppp yyouuuuuuu?"

And this guy was out like a race horse? FFFFFFTTTTTTT . . . out of the gate and onto the track. "Well, George," he said, speaking quickly, "I've gone to my people and I think we can offer you more. I think its going to be an opportunity (Blablablablabla)," and George, would go, "I'm sorry I don't feel right about this." See, the thing is, is when people speak to you the reason they speak the rate that they speak, most of the time has to do with the ability they have to process information normally. Now, it doesn't mean you cannot speed this process up. I know. I do it in seminars. I start out slower and I speed it up slowly and pretty much you can get people to process information more quickly. You also have to understand that this is only about consciousness. Because you can speak very fast and it will go in unconsciously. But unconsciously is not going to get somebody to meet with you to talk with you about changing their job. It's not going to get them to feel secure, because when it is just going in unconsciously the conscious mind isn't involved in things. What happens is people feel unnerved. Their unconscious is going "yes, yes" and their conscious mind is going "yeah, but . . . I could see myself, I feel off balance, I feel uncertain."

One of the primary rapport skills is that I want you to just open your ears up and you talk, listen to their intonation pattern. Listen to the counter predicates they use in language. Do they use a lot of picture words or a lot of feeling words or a lot of hearing words? Because you know it's that whole sentence that counts, "Well, it looks like a good opportunity but I feel that I am not ready for it."

Now, this means to tell you something about the sequence of how information is processed in this individual. There is no right or wrong in this. There is no good or bad. There is no diagnosis, tomorrow they might be different but it does give you the opportunity, if you listen to the intonation and if you listen to the sequence of how predicates fall out. I mean, do they have a tendency to use nothing but visual words, you'll get those. They'll come in and go well, "Yes, I've been *looking* for a new stereo." I mean I could really see how it would be something where we would have great evenings. We could listen to music." You can tell this is the kind of person that it's not going to even matter that much about what it sounds like. You are going to have to show them, and you are going to have to be careful where you put that because you don't want to put the picture in the wrong place. You want to put it in the right place, not in the not right place. Major thing.

Look at something, where you feel it is right and everything feels perfectly, versus where you have doubt. Where it just feels off kilter. Have you ever gone in and there is something and you want to buy it. And after you look at it with a person, something inside of you gave you the willies? Made you go, "Uh, it's just not right?" Or everything felt perfect, but when it was time to sign the contract . . . How many of you have had people that were just absolutely yes, yes, yes, and when you sat down suddenly there was doubt that hadn't been there? Like it came out of the blue.

Well one of the things we found, is that, for a lot of people, doubt is down right. And all the things they doubt and all the worries and their fears and stuff is, as we say down right important to them. Now what happens is that, if you sit somebody down at a desk and slide your contract right into that same place you can get them to doubt it in a cold second. Make sure that you use clip boards so you can have variety in where you place it and have them sign it. Now, it's not always in the same place for everybody but you want to be able to have ways of engineering each situation for yourself.

One of the tacks that I have taken with people, especially with large ticket items, is they say, "Well, I am here to look for a car." and I always go, "Well, I won't show you a car, right now. There is something more important we need to deal with first. Because I don't want to sell you the wrong car, I don't want to sell you a car that you can't afford. I only want to make sure that you understand my job is to make sure that you are making the right decision. Now, I know in the past there's times you've made the right decision, you've bought something and it's been perfect for you and you were totally satisfied. And there have been times where perhaps you've bought something and then afterwards weren't satisfied. It's my job to make sure you use your best judgment. So I want to ask you a couple of questions first. I want to ask you to think of a time where you were totally satisfied with something. You knew it was right and you were right." And I'll watch where their eyes move. Now people have told me that you can't do this with people. And I am here to tell you that I have done it in every situation from selling jets to people that don't speak the same language, to selling stamps. That is not stamps like the post office has. But stamps that are worth somewhat more money than that. Because they are unusual and old. Talk about a scam huh? Well these stamps aren't good anymore, and there aren't that many more around so they are worth more money, right. Why are they worth more money? Because, there aren't many of them around and there are people who will buy them. *Like you* for instance, you couldn't *buy now* figure out that *buy* and *buy* something will cross your mind. I love that phrase "cross your mind."

When you have people too set in their ways, you go, "Let's brain storm about this." That will always take them off the wall. They say, "What are you doing?" and you say, "Oh, nothing. That's it, just put it out of your mind." It's a great phrase. I want you to stop and think about other things. Have you ever had people that all of a sudden start shaking their head no? If they shake their head no, then the only thing to do is just mirror them and shake with it and start nodding yes. Sometimes they'll go right with you. It's always worth a shot, I figure. I like to breath at the same rate as people when I am dealing with them, too, especially on a one on one. And I breath with them and then I'll mirror them and start nodding my head yes, before I ask them questions. Because that way their head is already nodding yes. And I go, "Do you feel it's time to sign this contract?" and they'll go, "Yeah, I guess I do."

And I'll go, "Well not me, I'm not ready yet." And they'll go, "You're not?" And I'll go, "Nah. Not until I do something else."

Because the other thing I'd like you to do is to make a little list for yourself. Whatever it is that you do, you encounter a list of what's called "objections." We'll cover this later. What I want you to do first is to begin making a list of those you get in your business.

Now the next thing I want you to do is I want you to go back and find somebody else to do this next experiment with. It does require that you *use your behavior to induce the states,* but I want you to go through and find a time where they saw something and they wanted it, and they knew it. It was perfect. They made the right decision. Because what we are interested in here is not just where somebody bought something and loved it, but where they *had to make a decision* about it. Where they decided between several things and made the best decision, a decision they are satisfied with and have been for some time vs. where they bought something and they weren't satisfied with it. In fact they say things to you like, "Well, I knew better, but for some reason I just had to do it anyway." Now, I want you to have them think about one and think about the other and then have them go through and do both at the same time. (See Figure 1) Ask, "Is there a *difference?*" This is the magic word. Is there a *difference* between the location of the images? Is there a *difference* between which one is closer, or are they both the same distance, equal distance? Do you see yourself in both of them? Or do you see what you saw at the time, when you look at them? I want you to go through these because these are classic decisions. What you are going to do is to explore what's going on inside their mind that distinguishes a good decision from a bad decision. Cause the trick is you can get both of those, but when you sell somebody, when you negotiate a contract, when you do any of those things, and it goes through the bad decision one, you may feel clever but you will pay for it down the road. You will get buyer's remorse. You will get cheated, you will get no referrals, you may even get worse than that, you may get sued, you may get all kinds of things you don't want. Part of what you need to do if you are a really professional persuasion

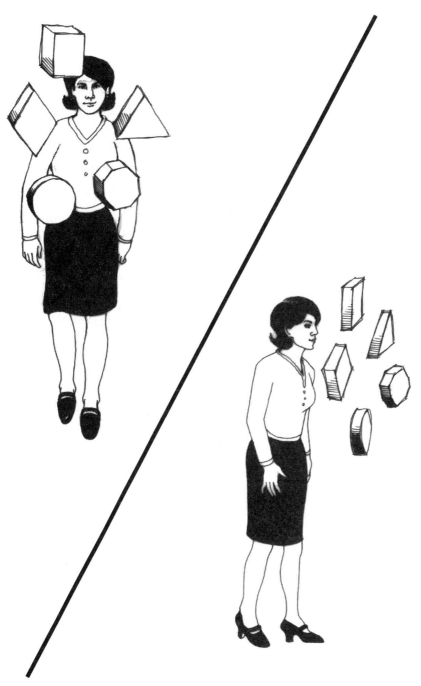

Figure 1

engineer is to distinguish in your own mind between the fact that both of these things exist in everybody.

Everybody makes good decisions and bad decisions and from our point of view it doesn't matter which is made when they make decisions somewhere else. But when they make decisions with us, we want them to be good ones. And you can engineer whatever it is that goes down, so that all their needs are filled. If they get a product that will service them, the one that they can afford, they'll be genuinely satisfied. Because if you sell people stuff that they can't afford, they will get mad at you down the road. They will blame you for everything. So, if you have them make good decisions, you'll always be better off. Now, I go to great lengths, you know, because the things that I sold, sometimes were very expensive. If they are very expensive the person can't really afford it in their world, I'll go inside and change their belief system about what their world is and how much money they can make. How many of you bought something that was more expensive, like a house, so you had to raise your income? And it worked. Well, if you do it deliberately, you can do it in sequence. See I like to raise my income before, it's just, you know, it works better for me. But, then I was the guy that wrote my term papers at the beginning of the semester. And then went on vacation and came back and then got paid for writing everybody else's. I wrote it in a little computer program and in those days, there were no computers around. But I happened to work in a lab where there was a computer. It wasn't my computer and I was supposed to do other things but I didn't like those things. So I wrote an algorithm by which I could write history papers and just pushed buttons and it would spew them out. So you know I would get the computer to knock these out, do a little editorial work, I'd have fifteen, twenty papers, just cruise out and I'd have a whole line of people waiting for them.

They were the people whose motivation strategy was the closer it got to the end, the more motivated they got. And there were some people who actually wrote the papers, they would stay up all night and then there were the ones that the closer it got to the end, the more they criticized themselves. And tried to find some other way. Since it was Stanford, they found a way of paying somebody else. There were some people at Stanford that didn't even go their classes, they hired somebody to be them. They didn't even go the first day, they would just show up at the frat house. They would hire some guy, his job was to be them for the year, go to all their classes, take all of their tests and the only thing they did was they went to beer busts. Think about it: some of those people are surgeons today. I know that, I was there, I wrote their papers. They got their Ph.D.'s and you know became very famous psychologists, some of which are published and well known. And they didn't go to their classes, and they didn't even write their thesis. All we did was put together the statistics. I wrote an algorithm so that it would vary all of the input, so that you were bound to get the right variance. By the way some of the famous research that is quoted on television, came out this program I wrote. You could put in any research project and it will make it so that it comes out right. So that any point of view your trying to prove will be proved, because it alters the data to fit the variant. All the time you would hear these famous quotes on the news and stuff, they say, "In the late 60's it was proven," don't believe it. Because you know what? There are guys pushing buttons like this all over the world. When people try to prove stuff to you with research, be very wary especially if it is about your health. But oooooh research, yeah yeah. That will move the picture right over. Well you might sell that to someone else but don't swallow it whole. Also, understand that a lot of other people don't, either.

Now what I want you to do is you go through . . . I am not asking you to change anything. There is nothing to change here.

All I want you to do is understand the difference and especially I want you to be able to move around so that you can sit at the side of somebody. I want you to move around a little bit and start imagining that this is out there inside their mind. That you actually get to walk around in somebody's mind by moving around them where they have put the pictures.

That means that if you don't like what is in a picture you can knock it out. Literally. People go, "Well . . ." I say, "Wait a minute." They go, "Huh?" You get to do things like if the picture isn't close enough you can get behind it and push it and that kind of stuff works all the time. I do it constantly. Now, I will show you a little something that I want you to try. I want you, when you find out where the thing is that they are delighted with, the good decision, so that if it was for them in one place . . . . I want you to actually walk around them and I want you take your hand . . . and this is the trick . . . and go curved to flat with you hand and back to curved as you touch their picture. So that you treat it as if it is real. FFFT . . . Great sound to make while you do it, by the way. All systems help. So the thing that is really a good decision for you is right here. So what we want to know is if the decision that you have made so far is really a good one. Because if we take this Mercedes and we put it in the same place as the good decision we want to know if it will stick. Does it feel like a good decision? See, you want be able to do things like, if they have it fixed in their mind that they have to have a station wagon or they have to have a big backyard . . . we could even take one side and pull it out a little bit and throw it away. Try on something new. Just to see if you can make yourself happier. You do want to be happier? Aren't those rhetorical questions wonderful? I love those things. We have people going "No, no I don't want to be happier. Not me. I was happy last year and look what happened. No more happiness for me." You never get that. Not once do I get that.

And I ask people, I say, "Do you want to feel good?" And they go, "Yeah." And I go, "Good. Let us take a look at this." Like that is related. But as long as you are congruent you can always connect everything together. Remember, people use this. This stuff by the way is called "junko logic." It comes from a man called George Paulu who wrote a book called "Patterns of Plausible Inference", where he studied what is credible in the human mind but doesn't make any sense at all. But when we hear it as human beings we go, "Wow, yeah!". And the fact that things are connected together are just that they occur in sequence one right after the other. We assume that they are related and that it doesn't matter what it was. You say, "Well, you want to be happy?" And they say, "Yeah, I want to be happy." "Well, then let us take this picture and move it away and put this one here and find out if you are." "Ya, let's do that. That makes sense." "Well good, then let's try it."

I know . . . you're saying inside your head, "I don't know if I can do this. What is it going to be this or this?" You will love doing this because you are going to discover that it is going on all the time. I mean I see wives go in and husbands and they look at a house and they say it is a great deal and they go back and forth and she will look at him and go, "I don't know. It sounds like a lot of money. Can you feel this?" as she touches him and he will go, "Yes, this is lot of money." Even though it is a great deal. You will have to watch for it because it comes at you from the other direction. The best way to become aware of it is to become a master of it and you can practice all day long everywhere you go. It is so much fun. You see my point? (with finger pointing) And something inside you goes, "Yes!", and even though you know it is going on, you still see my point, don't you?

Remember the purpose of this is to amaze yourself. Try little things, like taking the pictures of things and moving them backwards and forwards a little bit. Does it increase or decrease the state? You can make people more sure of a bad decision. They will go, "Well, I know it was wrong, I feel it was wrong." The picture is in one place and you can take the picture and make it bigger and move it up and closer and they will go, "Maybe it was the right thing." I'm not kidding. I want you to try this. When you put those hands behind it, move pictures a little closer, say, "Take a little closer look at this."

Use that phrase. I love that phrase, too. "Take a closer look at this. Can you feel this will be a good idea?" It is wonderful, what idea? I don't even have an idea and you're agreeing with me. Keep those ears open. It'll come out so fast that you will start listening because if you don't it will go inside and be there for the rest of your life. And then when you end up in therapy and you are going, "I don't know why I'm in therapy I just felt the need to come here. Seems I have this problem with my hand." That is the way it works. I taught a flirting class by the way just for the fun of it and it was the weirdest thing that ever happened. I literally had these people come and it was the quietest group. I thought they were going to come in to have fun but I got all these scared little puppies. I lined them up in a row and I put all the women on one side and all the guys on another. And I told the women that I wanted them to nonverbally either give a green light or a red light to the guy across from them and then what I wanted the guy across from her to do if it was a green light to hold up one finger if it was a red light to hold up two. And I had them do this and I said, "Now ladies, how many of the guys across from you got it right?" I had two hundred people in the line, three of them got it right. That is not a good statistic. And you know who these guys were dating?

You know who has the greatest opportunity to flirt is married couples. What surprised me was when I put this out, married cou-

ples thought they weren't allowed to go. I thought they'd be fill-
ing the place. "Oh, I'm sorry, we don't flirt. We are married." "I
beg your pardon." You know what that does, that builds in that
once-you-get-married-then-you-get-to-enjoy-life-less, less, less and
less. See this was a bad sales job. You want to make it so that
every time you look at what you decided to do you are happier and
more passionate about it. That includes what you do for a living.

❦ CHAPTER FOUR:
PRECISION ELICITATION

Let's face it, when you're in most of these business situations, how much time do you have to spend with a customer? I mean, sometimes, you can ask all the questions you want and sometimes you don't have much time. Also, there are many people who will give you all the information you need without you even having to ask for it directly. If you're in the everyday activities of any business, you know that there are sometimes too many times, or even too long a time when small talk occurs. When it occurs, I like to use it for its value to the process. What an opportunity to understand what's really going on.

Since "Linguistic" is our middle name, and language is one of the things we use to communicate what's going on inside our head, let's use this as an opportunity to learn to build new combinations of what you already understand on an intuitive level anyway. Because conscious understanding will enable you to unconsciously begin building new understandings of what to do and when, especially adding flex ability for your own communicating processes.

I like to point out that words are just words that can have more of an impact than you may have thought possible. In the Meta Model is a category called Modal Operators. Now think of these as the juices that rev up the action.

Now, I want you to play this sentence in your head, use your own internal voice for this. I find that if you do it out loud you never know who's around and may hear you and call the men with the white coats. Of course, if you do it inside your head so they can't hear you, then talking to yourself is OK, right? Use this as an example. Say:

- I *wish* I could take off Monday.

And notice the kinesthetics, the feelings of that statement and whether or not you feel strongly enough to do it. Now say the following, one at a time. What I want you to do is to stop after each one and notice the feelings you get and the difference from one to the other:

- I'd *like* to take off Monday.
- I *want* to take off Monday.

Notice the difference. These are just words. Now say:

- I *need* to take off Monday.
- I *have* to take off Monday.
- I *must* take off Monday.
- I *can* take off Monday.
- I *will* take off Monday.

Now notice the *differences* from one to the other by changing only one word! Now here is the even more interesting thing. Say:

- I'm *going to* take off Monday.

And notice the difference. Notice the feeling and whether the picture of the event is a movie or a still shot, color or black &white, the distance from you, do you see yourself in it or not, etc.

Notice whatever it is, and I want you to go do this with someone else, the action is around the verb *take* off. Now the interesting thing is that the best decision strategies that people make are movies and they include the following ingredients: meeting certain criteria which include very specific-to-the-individual voice qualities when describing those criteria. Those criteria are also driven by certain modal operators, of which the hierarchy of importance is primarily based on the modal operators driving those criteria. When a specific combination is made, the verb will go into an active mode and when the present tense of the verb is used, the intention for the action will change. Since time doesn't exist, only now exists, using the present form of the verb in the sentence will change the motivation for the action if it is planned to occur at a time description other than now. Another ingredient is that, people will more probably take action when they can see the movie run to the end, going through their options for more satisfaction and planning other activities around the event. These will also include information in the three major representational systems: kinesthetic, auditory and visual. So now let's do this all at once and say:

- I'm *taking* off Monday.

Notice what happens. If you had a slide, or still picture, it turns into a movie, it runs to the end and you plan what you will be doing Monday, don't you? You see, it's much easier to pay attention and use what's presented to you than it is to try to go inside your head and figure out whether someone fits into another meta description, like other sales programs use. I find that we don't have time during our everyday business to try to figure things out about what we think is going on inside someone else's head.

Your customer will always communicate what's going on and what the opportunity solutions are.

Now, if you were to say:

- I *should* take off Monday.

You'll again notice what happens to your own motivation. Oh well, that's the way it works. The most intriguing thing is that everyone may respond differently to any of these words.

I don't know why, but often people will come up to us in our seminars and tell us that they can't make pictures. Now we know that everyone uses all their senses, especially the three major ones and it's just a matter of how consciously aware they are over the control they have over their own processes. So this one time this guy comes up to us and tell us that he can't make pictures and was getting quite frustrated about this. The more interesting version of this is when they tell us that they can't make pictures as well as the other people they are working with. My question is, how do they know how well the other person is making them unless they can also see what the other person is doing and then making the comparison to their own?

After listening to this one person tell me about how he just went to another NLP seminar where he was told by the other seminar leader that he was just one of those people who wasn't going to be able to see his pictures, I said to myself. "What a bag of garbage that was." And now this guy was starting to build the belief about this. I decided to take the easy way out and I looked at him and said, "So you thought you couldn't *make pictures*?" and he says, "Yup." And his shoulders slumped, he lets out a short snort and begins to nod his head. I looked at him and said, "Well, I'm not going to ask you to *make a picture of anything*." He says, "Oh, good, because if someone else asks me to make a picture, I'm going to get real mad." And I said, "I want you to remember the most pleasant time you ever had as a youngster." He says, "OK, I remember once when I was a kid playing in my room with a new toy." I asked him, "What color is the room?" He says, "Green." I asked him to describe the room to me and he does. Not only is he describing what he sees, he shows me with his hands as he sculpts the room in front of him. Once he describes the room, I ask him if everything is clear to him and he says, "YES!", lets out a yahoo then continues on in the seminar. One of the things that ought to be clear is that when, as a communicator, you don't get the response you want, change what you're doing! This isn't a new idea, by the way, but I think that people tend to make things more difficult than they need to be most of the time.

As a professional communicator, salesperson, business person, or whatever, when you know where you're going it's easier to get there and when you get any resistance, it's easy to recognize as long as you're paying attention.

Ask one of your customers about "what are you *buying* today?", not what are they looking for, or other questions like this. There are certain things in the process that you *do* want to pre-suppose about the *action*, not the filters necessarily, so use unspecified (sensorily) language to find out where they are first. Whatever their response is, it will be full of valuable information about where you're going and how you can get there. Whenever you've bought something, you've gone through your own processes. Like, let's say you sell homes, for example. Your customer walks in and you start the conversation. They say, "Well, I'm looking for a new home," or "I want to talk about a new home," or "I want to walk through a new home," or whatever, this provides for the opening representational system as well as the road map with different avenues for you to use.

So you start the conversation and collect the information. I have a few trainees in sales who now, instead of sitting in their office waiting for the next person to show up and "it's their turn", stand by the windows and watch outside the building so that way, as potential customers drive up and step out of their cars, they often stop, look around and may even walk over to a few cars in the lot, or even to the model home next door, depending on the business. Maybe they look at different items in the store. Then the salesperson can walk up to them and she may say to them, "Hello, I'm Sue. I noticed that you were looking at the xyz model and the abc model . . . " Then they pause and wait for the response. Most times, the customer will describe what they want, the color, etc. and even give you more information than if you actually tried to elicit it. Do that. Even if it's not the business you're in or if you think you don't have the opportunity to do it. *Make the opportunity*. Whenever I find someone doing something that works I want to experiment with it. I'll even go into other people's businesses to find out. You know, even retail stores, or whatever.

So you start the process, and *open your eyes and ears and all your senses* and begin to map out the information as they present it to you. Have you noticed how many people talk with their hands? Know why? Because they do and when they do that, they show you their map. They'll point out their favorite places to put information, they point out their time and space relativity, and they'll even show you how they disregard information by pushing it away with their hands. And the sounds they make when they do this. OOOOOOOOOH what a wealth of information! You know some of the sounds: Hrmph, snort, nah, tsk tsk, Ahhhhh, Mmmmm, Ahh Haaaaa, and others.

It's like, maybe you've learned to paraphrase back to people things they say as a way of letting them know you understand them. What an insult! I mean if you think about something that's important enough for you to want and let's say you call it *"Fun."* Is *"Fun"* and "a *good time"* the same? Probably not, and they're probably in different locations on your map, right? Some of you may say, "Well they're sort of the same," which means they're not the same. Let's start going for precision hear. So, paraphrasing is some convoluted way of trying to let the other person know that you think you understand enough of what they're saying and that you can actually help them. This is not the best way to build "yes" responses. If you want to build sort of responses or could be responses, then ok, but we want to build "YES." Why even go near resistance? No sense makes this!

Think of paraphrasing in a new way. I call it "parrot phrasing." Most people will teach you how to not match so well so that you aren't mimicking someone or making fun of them and I agree, if you have other than good intentions. Your customer is paying you for results, not to screw with them. It isn't something that you do all the time, everyday. You do it when you want to test that you got it right and to demonstrate you're understanding. Just like anything else, too much of anything can be too much.

So when you know what you're doing and you're congruent and you have a way of knowing how you're doing, then precision is best. People go, "But doesn't that take lots of practice?" And I'll tell you what, after teaching this for years, I can tell you that it's not something new you're learning to do, unless you've never learned how to open your eyes and ears, and all your senses. "Parrot phrasing" is about delivering back exactly, did I say that right? EXACTLY and PRECISELY what you hear and see, I mean the hand demonstrations, and everything. That's everything, of course, that's *useful to the process*. Why anyone would want to match back sneezing, confusion, or distaste in the selling process when selling your products or services is . . .

Also, you don't have to repeat everything they say, only the responses that you know are of value to them . . . How do you know this?

Now one of the reasons why precision is so important here is that everything has it's place to fit back into. The sentence structure and their hand mapping will demonstrate that to you each and every time.

I hear so many times when well intentioned sales people ask a simple question like, "What do you *want* in the (product or service)?" And the response comes like . . . "I need this, want these and would like to have these other things . . ." And the salesperson gives them all back as *needs*. Or they may even ask for their *needs* first, which may or may not be the best place to start. Think about it. Some people say, "Oh, you're just using semantics." And I go, "Yeah, what's wrong with that?" After all, we are talking about communication here, aren't we? Or they go, "You're trying to put words in my mouth," and I say, "No, I'm trying to get them to come out."

So when thinking modal operators, for example, wants, needs, and like to haves, have each their own time and place. (Remember the exercise in Chapter 3?) Think of them as: in the order of importance for most people. I mean, even if you have five *wants*, they can be placed in order of importance, but how many of you really have time to sort through this? Sometimes there's entirely too much information, it seems that way, at least, that we as selling professionals have to sort out. "Let's keep it simple and powerful," I always say. I mean, less is more. Why build roads that we don't need? Why not use the ones that are already there and use them for racing for fun and profit?

Take this example where the lady comes into this showroom and is looking to buy a new kitchen. The saleswoman says to her, "Hi, I'm Linda . . ." greeting the woman. The woman says, "I'm just looking right now, you know, just shopping around, for a new kitchen. I'm not sure where I'm going to buy it, yet, I'm just looking." So Linda says, "Well you, like me, don't look like someone who just settles for any old thing. I mean, it looks to me that your kitchen is very important to you. And I wouldn't sell you just any old kitchen, so what's your new kitchen going to be like because we only will sell you the kitchen that will thrill you each and every time you look at it!"

Now the customer begins to walk through the showroom and stops and begins to describe her kitchen:

"I *need* to have lots of storage space for my pots and pans, I have lots of different pots and pans, you know. And I *need* counter top space to work on. I *want* wood cabinets, maybe oak, and I *want* the doors to the appliances to match the cabinets. I also *want* indirect lighting and I'd also *like to have* some built in items, you know, like a mixer, the instant hot water thing. Yeah, those would really be nice." And the whole time she's explaining this, she's showing Linda exactly where all these things are right there in front of her. And then Linda says to her, "Ok, let me see if I got this right. You need lots of storage space, you need counter space to work on, you want wood cabinets, maybe oak, and the appliance doors to match the cabinets. You want indirect lighting and you'd also like to have some built in items in your new kitchen." All the time, Linda's also redrawing the map right there in front of this woman! And this woman looks at Linda and goes, "You've got it! (This is the music of success, what a powerful response since this customer didn't know where to buy.) You know, I've been looking for some time now and you're the first person who understands exactly what I'm looking for. You haven't even tried to talk me into something I really don't want. Do you think you can help me to build my new kitchen?" Now Linda says to her, get this, "Yes, I think we can build your new kitchen because we know exactly what you're looking for. And we want you to be thrilled with your new kitchen. Now, let's go into a few more details so we can fill in the other pieces to this picture for me your kitchen as I start to sketch it out here to give to your designer, who will then figure out all the precise dimensions of everything." Now I thought this was great but Linda didn't stop there. She asks this woman if she wants to go with stock cabinets, or custom designed. Of course the woman asks what's the difference. I thought that Linda was about to create her first own objection for this deal when she said, "Well, of, course, custom design is a little more money, but, the price difference is so insignificant when you get exactly what you're looking for, after all." This woman looks at her and says, "Let's take a look at the custom designed cabinets first." This is priceless, as most of these opportunities can be. Think about how many times time and price, the two major objections, or excuses, as the case may be, are only excuses. How many times have you gone out to buy something with a specific price in mind and you spent more for the item than you even had budgeted anyway? Another ten to fifteen thousand on a home or another three or four thousand for a car? And only because you "*felt right about the deal or the salesperson!*" Think about it. So getting the customer to "*feel right*" is a valuable selling objective.

As a general guideline, we know that people like guidelines and procedures. Sometimes guidelines aren't useful and sometimes they are. When they are used to get you started, you see, then you develop your own set of skills so you drive your own bus because you learn how to use what's going on around you as your guideline. So, I like to gather up about maybe four, five or six things before "parrot phrasing" them back. If they give you one, and you give it back, and they give you another, and you give it back, and do that four or five times, they'll look at you real funny.

The local business chamber had called me to ask if we would be interested in a price comparison on some insurance. We're a member of this business group so I said sure. So this guy calls me up a few weeks later from this insurance company and says, "I understand that you're looking for insurance." This is not the best way to start. I, of course realized that someone, somewhere screwed this up so I said, "Well, not exactly. Someone asked me if I would be interested in a comparison and I said, sure." And this guy says to me, "Well that's not what I was told. When can I meet with you? I said, "You can't. I'm too busy. Send me the information so I can look at it. Then, if I like what I see, we can sit and talk more." The guy says, "We don't do it that way. We have to make an appointment and sit face to face." I said, "I'm really too busy for that right now. It would really be better for me if you could send me the information first so I could look at it. Then I'll call either way, whether I like the comparison or not, and let you know if we can get together." This guy says, "I just told you we don't do it that way." I reached down into the depths of my understanding and said to him, "I'm too busy right now." He asks if he can call me in a few weeks and I said sure. Hey, I figured, maybe he'll get it and just send me the information first, then call. Well today he calls and the first thing out of this guys mouth is, "Hi, this is Sam, you told me to call you today." I said, "because you asked if you could. . . so what can I do for you?" He asked me again if I had twenty minutes I could give him. I repeated my request for the information and this guy says to me, get this, "Do you have an insurance license?" I said, "I'm the customer, I don't need one." This guy loses it and starts yelling something about blowing that stuff past other people but not to do it on him so I didn't as I clicked down the receiver. I'll bet business is tough for him. I mean, I was really looking for a comparison, what with the prices all over the place today, but, now neither he nor the company he works for will ever get my business, someone else will. Maybe it will be Linda.

Sometimes I do enough seminars in a row that sometimes I even forget. I'll get up after it is all over the next day and I'll come down and sit by myself. Actually one time I did something like 75 seminars that were either 1 or 2 days all over the country on this what I refer to as a psychocircus tour. They had Gregory Bateson and Buckminster Fuller and Ashley Montegue and all these people and we would all go into a city and they'd run 3 days for the people that were there and we would go on Friday to one city, Saturday to the next, Sunday to the next and do an hour. I kept doing this going around the country and when it was finally over I flew to meet a friend of mine in Houston and I actually got up in the morning and put on a suit and went downstairs just like an automatic on program. It is easy for human beings. One thing that we learn quickly is a rut. We are masters of that. Virginia Satir once told me, she said, "The will to survive is not the strongest instinct in human beings. The strongest instinct in human beings is to do what is familiar." And that is part of what makes it hard for us is that we learn something that works to some degree then we have a tendency to just keep doing it and even when it doesn't work, do it with people. What we try to do is increase the volume to get it to work. I've noticed this when I go to foreign countries and there are other Americans there. They will walk in and they will go, "Can you tell me where the bathroom is?" And the person will go, "No English." And they will raise their volume and go "CAN YOU TELL ME WHERE THE BATHROOM IS?" And they will go (loudly) "NO SPEAK ENGLISH." And they will go even louder **"CAN YOU TELL ME WHERE THE BATHROOM IS?"** As if volume will break the language barrier.

One of the things I want to do with elicitation is, actually two things I want to accomplish and one I refer to as "Attitude Adjustment."

I've noticed that some of you, not all of you, some of you are just a little too nice. Now being nice is fine but there is a difference between being nice and making it so. Some people just do things that make me wince. For me, the ones that make me wince are the ones that have bad tonality. It is not even that I can't sell them something it is just that the question is how fast can you do it without having your eardrums break. I had a lady who is from Long Island who probably had the worst tonality of any human being on the planet. She spoke like a dental drill. When she came in she said, "Oh look at that car. I want one of those." And the inside of my teeth began to hurt. All the nerves in every tooth I ever had where shimmering. I walked up and knowing my own principles and wanting to try them, I turned around and I looked at her and (with her tonality) I said, "Do you really want to buy a car?" And she turned around and said, "Where are you from?" And I said, "Long Island." And she said, "Oh, I knew this was my lucky day." And I said inside my head, "Well it sure in hell isn't mine." Sometimes you have to get that line inside your head so that it just doesn't fly out of your mouth. But she had a husband that looked like he had been punished by a bad tonality his whole life. He was walking around behind her and he was like shoulders slumped and he going, "Okay, Mildred anything you say, Mildred." And she was going, "Let's get this one." And he went over at the window sticker on the car and I could see his heart go "ah, ah, ah, ah." He almost keeled over on the spot. And I told him, "Stop that. Take a deep breath and just feel good." And I put my hand over his ears and she said, "What are you doing?" I said, "Oh it is a magic trick." I'm going to make that headache that has been there for 70 years go away. I said, "Now, say inside your head, I'm ready to get this." I opened my hands and he went, "Oh, I'm ready to get this."

Now I want to teach you a couple of other things because I don't know if you've noticed that human beings do not listen well. Have you noticed that? Don't be ashamed because most human beings don't really know much about hearing. Your ability to hear, in what we do, especially those of you working on the telephone, by the way.

There is a lot of people who think they hear well and I got news for you. I'm just feeling like I'm getting started. Everyday I start learning to hear more and more stuff. For example one of the things that I noticed for those of you who had some NLP training. Remember all of that stuff with the equations those guys do who were stuck at various levels of my development? I meet these people on planes and it is so much fun or in airports and places because they are always going through reading one of my books and writing equations out on paper and I think, "Poor soul. I'll help him." So I walk up and I go, "Hey, what is that about?" And they usually look at me and say, "It is very complex you wouldn't understand." You see, it wasn't until recently I put a picture of mine on the book, my publisher actually snuck that on behind my back. Because it deprives me the opportunity to go and test things like this. For example some years ago I was on my way to teach a sales training course in Dallas, Texas. Flying from San Francisco I sat down and when I sat down on the plane I was going to sit back and relax but as I put my chair back and looked over there it was . . . the cover of <u>The Structure Magic</u> staring back at me and I peeked over and I looked at this guy and this guy had this look on his face like he could eat shoe leather in a cold second. His ability to stick his foot in his mouth would be unmatched. So I asked the guy. I looked over at him and I said, "Are you a magician?" And the guy looked at me and said, "Of course not." Like I could tell. He is reading a book called <u>The Structure of Magic</u> and that is where you find <u>The Structure of Magic</u>, by the way . . . in the occult section. Because every time I go into a book store that is where it is . . . right there in the occult section, where it belongs. So I said to this guy, I said, "If it is not about magic what is about?" And he said, "It is about language." And he said, "It is very complex and . . . ." And I said, "Well, I'm a pretty smart guy. Why don't you explain it to me?" And he told me, "It takes years of training to be able to understand this." And then he told me, which was a major mistake, he said, "I'm a certified clinical psychologist." And I went, "No shit." This is how you begin the constipation induction. See I practice these things because, you see, to me your ability to use language to begin to induce a state . . . one of the ways to practice is to be able to induce "involuntary responses." Goose bumps is a good one. If you could talk about situations where certain things occur you can actually be able to get the responses that go with them. It is only a four hour flight from San Francisco to Dallas that day. He had so many involuntary responses that he went unconscious after a while. Just don't know what happened. But you see, I stood up and I went to the bathroom after a while, after this guy condescendingly explained to me how <u>The Structure of Magic</u>, how "questions that you can listen . . ." Actually he didn't say "listen" he said you could *see* the surface structure of sentences and it tells you what to challenge inside of people and I went, "Gee, I wrote the book and it doesn't make any sense to me." And I looked back at him and I said, "Well, how do you *see* the surface structure of a sentence?" And I looked in the book and, since I wrote it, I know what is there sometimes. And linguists did an interesting thing. They do it this way. They say there is deep structure and surface structure. Now if you look at <u>The Structure of Magic</u>, I don't know how many of you have read it, but there are three appendixes in there. Because *The Structure of Magic* was actually my dissertation. And the three appendixes the . . . first one is called "System Simple", and it is a big thing full of math and the second one is called "System Deep", and the third one is called "System Trance." I was out to get my professors, believe me. If you read the equations it even goes deeper and deeper still. So as you go through the equations in the thing, as it goes down the page it teaches you how you go from the unconscious communication to the conscious communication so that as you look down you can see how deep you can go inside yourself. It is the kind of thing that says, well if you can induce a state of confusion in people you can induce in them almost anything. Now a lot of times people are very good at getting rapport but we are going to run through a couple of other things. One of them has to do with your ability to switch the way in which you speak. So that you can mirror someone else. Not just sympathetically . . . so that you can actually run around and try different representational systems to be able to describe something completely visually, completely kinesthetically so that you can switch the way in which you do it.

But for our purposes here, I want you to begin to realize that each and every statement that you make has an impact. So I want you to try some of the simple confusion techniques that I use. I know that others refer to this kind of stuff as pattern interruptions. I'm a little more blatant about things than others, if you can imagine that, but in a subtler kind of way. Instead of having people go "Oooooohh", like that, I do it for them and as they are going up I am telling them to close their eyes and relax. Because I want to confuse them only about what it is that their beliefs are at a moment in time.

Clients are going to say to you, in the course of your conversation with them, the following thing, and I always want you to hear it. They're gonna go, "uh huh," Do you know what that means? That means that they didn't hear a thing you said. And they go, "uh huh, um, yeah, uh huh. Um hum." Always take that as something where you back up because it means that they've already got a picture in their mind and they're just not gonna let you change it, and they're gonna go, "uh huh" until they get a chance to tell you about it. So you might as well stop then and realize that you're not getting information through to them. The following sounds are the magic cues that what you're saying is going inside. When you tell them something and they go, "ooohhh, aaahhh," this is one of the best. Ummmmm, because all of those things are the sounds that start accessing in the mind. Think about it. If somebody says, "Well, what movie do you want to see tonight?" and you go, "ummmm. Then you're gonna go and think of one." If you look at somebody and you say, "Well, what's on your mind and they go, hummmmm." It's real different than if they go, "Well, uh , hum, ah, ah," you know that what's on their mind isn't gonna be good. It's really important for you to realize that you want to keep them active in the process and the reason I use so many rhetorical questions is I want them to feel yes coming up. Yes coming up. To me, the more questions you can ask where you get yes answers, not um hum answers, not ah huh, answers—you go, "Do you want a good stereo?" and if they go, "Uh huh," then you didn't present it to them in a way which struck their soul. Cause to me when I say okay, you came in here to buy a stereo, the question is, do you just want a stereo? Cause you can get a boom box. Actually, you could just buy one that's empty without equipment that would look nice as furniture. Or "Do you want to have music that surrounds you, something that looks beautiful in your house and something that goes in your ears and over your skin. Because those speakers right now are bathing you in sound and you want that sound to be perfect, clear and clean. Something that you'll, every time you look at it, know you can feel good at any moment, cause it's not just music, it's something that changes your mood. You want your mood to be bathed in static or do you want to be able to go into sensuous states, or excited states, anytime you want. That's called a compound statement, by the way. Don't think about stereos, think about the compound statement now.

Because when I present it to them, I'm going through each and every one of their sensory systems, building something that's sumptuous, something that's desirable. And this is true in you're selling consulting. This is true of everything, you know. Do you want things in your business to keep running along in the same old groove until it just digs down in the dirt and you all burn out, and one of you has a heart attack and you all live in regret? Very rarely do you get, "Uh huh?" Yeah, yeah, yeah, that's what we're up to. Yeah, well, of course not. You go, "Is that like yes?" Very important. Is that like yes. Now without the variation in tone and without your ability to use your voice resonantly . . . because the truth is, every time you speak to somebody the sound doesn't just jump into their ears. In fact, the most important part of communication is the tone.

Can't you say no and mean yes? Yes and mean no? Very easily. Well, you know, "You want to go down and buy a Mercedes?" "Yeah, sure." Sure, like when when hell freezes over.

Now, if you can beef up your attitude and beef up your ability to hear things, because those very accessing sounds . . . I found out sometimes I just make them for them. I can go, "Are you interested in having the quality of your life be better?" And as their eyes begin to move, I go, "Hmmmmmmm." They'll go and shift and I'll go, "Ahhhh." Now, your ability to be resonate in your tonality . . . and I want to teach you a little trick here and I do this in public speaking courses, but I want to do it here, too. I want you to know what it feels like to have your voice resonate. That way you'll recognize it in others, too.

So, put your feet on the floor, we're gonna do a little vocal exercise. That's right, clear your throat and go, "Ahhhhhhhhh." Get it out of your system. That's right, it's good for your throat. I know whenever I say, "I want you to sound really good, there's always—aaaahhhh." It's real easy. Now, the first trick is, before you make a sound, I want you to breathe in because a lot of people forget that, and they go, "Gaaakeeehhhh," as they run out of breath and that's why it goes like that. So you inhale and take the air in, and then I want you to do this: I want you to take two fingers and place them on your nose, and you don't have to press hard or hit yourself or anything and go, "This is my nose." Move them down to your lips and say, "This is my mouth." Place them on your throat and say, "This is my throat." Place them on your chest and say, "This is my chest." Place them just below your sternum and say, "And if I speak from here, I'll quadruple my income. And get much sex whenever I want."

Yeah, I know. People say, "You seem to have your mind on money and sex," and I go "Yeah, Ohhhhhhh . . . Money. Ohhhhhhhh, Sex and Fun. Ummmmm hmmmmmmmm." Can't leave that out because to me it's the propelling driving force of the universe. It's the ability to find out you can turn *anything* into fun. I had one guy in a seminar, he raised his hand, and he went, "Dr. Bandler, um, I work for a company" with that drilling tone - that is exactly the way he sounded, too by the way. I love these people, I memorize 'em, photograph em, learn them so I can be an idiot, too. I'm saving that for my retirement. When I have all the money I want then I'm gonna use these behaviors to make sure I don't make any more. And he goes, "I work for a company and all we sell is fencing, and uh, there are lots of people that sell fencing, uh, how can people get excited about fencing?" And I looked at him and I said, "Well, I can get reeeal excited about fencing," and I said, "Don't you *believe* fences are good?" And he goes, "Yeah, but, one fence is no better than another." And I said boy, there's real faith in the product, huh. I said, "Well, to me, you have to understand that the most important thing to me is that somebody opens the door, looks at that fence and they feel wonderful, otherwise, they're not gonna send you new clients. They're gonna have 'em go to any old fencing company. They're not gonna look outside and realize the fence is a sense of security. It's a sense of privacy, it means you can stand next to it naked and no one will know. It means that your animals and your children won't wander off till they get older." And what is it about it? You know, the dog learns to go under the fence and the kids learn to go over it. Right. Now, I also discovered a little trick, I said, "For me, you know, I want to walk into work and look at my product and feel wonderful. Most people just sell fences. What if you could sell a fence and a good feeling with it, that people could take with them and have for the rest of their life?" And he looked at me and said, "Wow." And I said, "Now, are you interested in buying some fencing?" And he went, "Yeah." And I said, "Good. Then buy it from yourself." He forgot in that moment what he was doing, because he was so bathed in tonality that came from here, your chest. Now if you're bent over and if you're crooked and you don't realize sound is created from your entire movements then you won't get the results..

Everything you do with your body. You need to open up your body and be able to look at somebody and realize that you want to project the sound, that it doesn't just come from your mouth by the way, it comes from your chest. It seeps all over a person so that when you look at them and you say things, I like this, "Well, today I want to be honest with you." Right? Now the only way you can say something that stupid is if you're inside making pictures of how you're not gonna have enough money to pay your bills at the end of the month because you have to plan for that sort of thing, you know, otherwise it won't happen. I see people walk into stores and watch sales people drive them away. It's unbelievable to me. I watch people come in . . . why do you think they come into a car lot? Right! To buy a car. People come in and they go, "Uh, can I help you?" and people will go, "Just looking." And I always finish the sentence — and go," . . . at your future automobile." Why not? They started the sentence, I get to finish it. It's only half a thought. I'll decide where the rest of it comes from. I always look at that as an opportunity. Everybody else I know walks away from it. They're not a puma. They're not there with their nails out. I don't walk up and go "Can I help you?" I walk up and I say, "Are you looking to do something intelligent?" I never have people look at me and go, "Nah, I'm just out to do stupid stuff today. I'm trying to feel like a teenager, you know."

It's like, think of the things human beings are willing to do, and I want you to think this through just for a moment. I know some of you do these things, I don't want you to take it personally. Human beings put on two sticks, ski down and jump off of a mountain for fun.

Think about it, somebody said, "Hey, you can come down and buy this stuff and jump off of a mountain." People went, "Wow, give me a pair of those, I'll jump off the mountain, too." Think about this. People with boats. You have to buy a boat so somebody can drag you behind it on a pair of sticks. I think this is really incredible. They used to call it keel hauling years ago, it used to be punishment. But now, people learn to do tricks on the back. In fact, if you're good at it, you can do it with only one ski and if you're great at it, they don't even give you the skis they just drag you behind the boat on the rope. People go out and spend enough money to buy a boat and the stuff. Right. You used to go out and insult somebody and they'd drag you behind the boat, now you have to go out and spend the money to — and you have to get a really fast boat so you can get dragged really well. There are people who jump out of airplanes for fun. Deliberately. They go, "Well, what do you want to do today?" And you go, "Hell, let's jump out of an airplane." There's an idea. Now, if all of these things could be made - and human beings when they do it, they are having fun - this means that we need to stop and consider what we can make enjoyable.

So I'm gonna ask you to try a little sales. I want to stop here with you selling an idea to someone else, a friend or partner. And I want that idea to be that you build in those beliefs that we talked about. That the tougher it is to sell something to somebody, the more fun it is. Cause if you walked in and they go, "I want that," and you give it to 'em, that's kind of boring, it takes the play out of it. The more stubborn they can be, the more stubborn you can be. Now, you remember the exercise you did earlier with the sub-modalities where you elicited the thing. What I want you to do is to pull that page out again, only this time, I want you to get all the submodalities that go with the powerful belief. Things like, do you believe breathing is good? Something basic, do you believe the sun is coming up? I want you to find out the location of where they position that belief, and then what I want you to do is, in your most smooth tonality, in your best presentation that you can make and in every representational system, I want you to have that person consider 3 new ideas: 1) That challenge is fun; 2) that you can sell to anybody or convince anybody of anything. Now it doesn't matter that it's not true, but if you have that belief, it means you'll do it with every fiber of your muscles and your soul. Now, the way I want you to do it is I want you to make it fun. I don't want you to sit down and do that hard core stuff. I want you to walk up and say, "Hey, do you believe the sun is coming up tomorrow?" Watch where their eyes move. If not, say, "Well, do you see a picture in your head? Do you have a voice that says yes or no?" Sounds a little bit like schizophrenia. But everybody does it. You have to know what you believe and what you don't believe. Soon as you know where that image is, ask them how big it is. Is it like this, is it like that? When you localize it, I want you to walk around and get behind it, see, because I have an idea for you. I want to pull out this picture, (wisssss) that says challenge is fun. "Can you see this?" As soon as they say "Yes", go, (ffffff) put it right there where the strong belief is. Now, it might seem like well, adults don't normally do that, hell I did it in a Mercedes lot. And there's a $3K commission. I don't know about you, I'm willing to act a little foolish. They won't think it's offensive, not when they're laughing. Not when they say, "What did you do?" and you go, "Ahhhh, just pasting up new ideas, it's just something I'm trying out here." It may seem silly, but you know, do you like to enjoy yourself? Nay, not me, I hate to enjoy myself. I don't like that. It's — I don't feel authentic if I'm enjoying myself. It's only through pain, that you can change. Do you believe this? Somebody sold that idea! Only through pain you can change. Hell, come on over here, I'll whack you a few times on the side of the head. It'll be good for ya. Maybe you'll get some sense in then.

Now, as you begin to build new pathways in your own brain, so that your flexibility increases proportionately to your desire to learn, really learn, we want you to write out the ambiguities, at least the scope, syntactic, and phonological. You see, the Milton Model, contrary to what most people think, is used for more than just your "official" hypnotic work. There's one for you: "official" hypnotic work, as if there's any other kind of trance than those that you're in any way. I mean think about it. The thing about trance is that it's just about altering states, which means a state other than the one you're in just before this one. So it's just a matter of whose trance you're in, where and when. But when you can generate language patterns more elegantly, you can generate more than you thought possible. Your senses are keener, sharper and you'll see and hear things you didn't even know have been there all along.

So I want you to begin with the ambiguities: phonological, scope, syntactic and punctuation. Take the first and write down one hundred or more. That's write 100 or more. Because I want you to say them and write them down. Over the next few days, I want you to do this because this is one way of learning quickly. Come up with as many as you can as quickly as you can at first. If you find yourself laughing at them, that's great because humor is the brainchild of creativity. Get yourself to laugh and find the humor in things and others will, too. Especially when you know what you're doing. So start with funny logical ambiguities and write them down. There must be a zillion of them out there. Write out all versions of the same one, there may be two or three or more. Even if there spelled the same and have a different meaning, write them down for each meaning you find. Then I want you to run these past your friends and have fun with them. They may find others for you. Write them down.

I mean, just think about it, everything we can do with structuring sentences and directing stories is a matter of the fact that these are all built from just twenty-six letters of the alphabet. That's it. Just twenty six letters and there are five of them that cost you something. Just twenty-six letters can result in the combinations necessary to create specific meanings. The possibilities are endless, especially when your breaking rules straightens things out.

There are explanations in the back of the book about these things to help get you started. The important thing is that you do it now, why wait? Some examples for the phonological ambiguities are: right, rite, write; check, check; rain, reign; etc.

Some of you may be thinking, well gee, these are nice but, how do they apply to business? Well, I'll tell you that first of all, when you think about all the words you say all day long anyway and how many sentences, then are you really getting the biggest bang for your buck?

We had this woman in one of our business seminars, her boss sent her. Now she came because she wanted to be able to increase her rate of collections against their receivables and this was a professional office, like a dentist, or chiropractor, or something. Well, anyway, what she started doing is: when the client was ready to leave, looks at them, puts out the palm of her hand and starts to open the appointment book as she says, "We need a check . . . on your next appointment." She holds her hand out while she's look-ing through the appointment book. Now the clients ask "How much do I owe you today?" She tells them, they write out the check and they make another appointment all at the same time. She's been doing this now for about four years and she's absolute-ly delighted with it and so is her boss. Hey, receivables are down, so's the phone bill, by the way, and business is up because people are also making their next appointment. The state is that most of them are already feeling pretty good at that time because they're relieved of whatever pain they were in, etc. The point is that she is being more successful beyond what she thought possible and she thinks it's great. The humor of it alone keeps her going and she's been finding more ways to use humor by using ambiguities more and more every day. So much for serious business tech-niques.

Then generate some syntactic ambiguities. Generate as many as you can at any one time, Maybe fifty or more and write them down. I like organizing principals. Some of these will be using phonological ambiguities. So come up with as many as you can in as short a time as you can. You can't get enough of this. It's what humor is all about, not jokes. You know, make those pow-erful distinctions between jokes and humor, there is a difference, you know.

Write down as many scope ambiguities as you can come up with just like the others. These are really useful in this business because of the way you can use these to change meaning elegant-ly. There are lots of well known ones out there that are really good examples, as one liners like, "I caught an elephant in my paja-mas." This one guy I know sold this big ticket item to a woman wearing red shoes and glasses. Things have never been the same with either of them. Write down as many as you can in as a short a period a time as possible. By now you're probably noticing that you're using combinations of ambiguities already. Have fun!

See, I want you to think about selling trance as how to communicate using the fullest range of possible communicating choices. Punctuation ambiguities are next and here is what I want you to do: as you write these down use all the ambiguities and keep the punctuation ambiguity going in the right direction is easy when you think about racing cars and ideas since the time goes by now I want you to realize that your investing in your future now and then some more.

So write, again, so this time you're finding it easier and easier to use more and more flexibility in how you say what you say because we want to move on to some of the other patterns here. Use rhythm, a have fun attitude, a full range of voice inflection, subtlety, and remember, it's not about being slick, that's easy. Persuasion is about helping people make the right decision.

Now because you want to be able to make distinctions in your brain about moving people in directions and locations of things, time and space predicates are important and are relative in nature.

For example, I said to you or you said to me that you are *going to* do something. Think about something that you are *going to* do. And since time doesn't exist except for now, then we represent time using space.

I was sitting on an airplane one time with this associate and we were flying back from a business deal in Florida. And I was reading this book called <u>Using Your Brain For a Change</u>. I was reading it for the nine millionth time. Well, this guy asked me, "What are you reading?" And I said, "A book." (Of course, I'm the one with the attitude.) And I am looking at this here book and he goes, "So, what's the name of it?" I looked at him and I said, "<u>*Using* Your Brain, For a Change</u>." I couldn't resist. And he asked, "What is it about?" I said, "Well, it's all about learning how to <u>Use *Your* Brain For a Change</u>, like for example, suppose you want to make a specific decision about something or you want to be able to learn how you think in words or pictures and things like that." And he goes, "You can help me with a decision? I'm going to make a decision." Now, that was an interesting invitation. So I sat there and realized that he already made it because he didn't say he was deciding on something. He said, "So you can help me with a decision." Which means he can already recognize it as a nominalization as an event that will already occur and has not yet. This is what I get to do in business. People say, "You are playing with words." I go, "Yup. Isn't it great?"

And as I'm reading this thing he says, "You can help me with a decision?" And I said, "Sure, which one?" And he said, "Well I've been making this decision now, for a while." And inside my head, I go, "Right, you've already made the decision. You just haven't implemented it yet or executed it." But I didn't say that to him. I said, "Well when you think about this decision, where is it?" Now by the way, actually his words were, "I'm going to make a decision," I complete his sentence "happen."

Now, think about something that you are *going to* do, point to where it is. Now, think about something you *are* doing. Point to where that one is. It's in a different location, isn't it? Closer, bigger, brighter?

Well, this guy had an interesting one because here's what I figured out about how he was doing it. I said to him, "How often have you been going to make this decision, since whenever you decided to do it?" And he said, "Oh, a couple of years now." And I go, "What happens?" He goes, "Well, I'm going to probably be making it in about two weeks." Two weeks doesn't exist. And I asked, "Where is it?" And he said, "Well it's . . ." and he showed me on his timeline the location and he goes, "Well it's right about here," He moves his hand out at about a 45 degree angle and about arms length away, the picture of the decision was just beyond where his hand was, you know, just out of reach, so to speak. And I said to him, "Well let's go to tomorrow just for a moment, in your mind. Where's the decision?"

Get this, the decision kept moving along each day. He would move a day and the decision would move a day. Sales people wouldn't be interested in this. And I said, "And what about the next day?" He said, "Well, it just seems to go to the next day." Now it's only because of listening to the way that he sequenced his sentences and the words that he used, and me actually getting inside of the way that he was describing it, so I could understand his experience. This was in a pretty quick moment. This guy's decision kept moving each day and he kept, according to his words, "Putting it off." Now to make it even more interesting, when he showed me this, he kept *putting it off his timeline* to the side. This is not a good decision executing place. Have you ever noticed that? People, whether they're in business or not, make decisions but don't execute them? I think this is a great strategy for procrastination and maybe for things that you never really want to do, but for making things happen? I don't think so.

It's in the language, tonality and the physiology. The thing is to understand hear where the process is going in the conversation and what they are describing and whether or not you want them to consider it now or have them already have had considered it at another time so that you can now use it as a resource now from then. Resources, those experiences that include usefulness come from the past, or is it passed, can be applied in language, especially since your brain works faster than you think.

So if it's a decision that they think they haven't made, yet, although they already have and they just don't know it, then having them think about something when they think they are going to think about it but doing it now and having already done it is one way of taking a future experience into the experience of now, enjoying it and having it become a resource. And it is in the language.

How many of you get people who go, "Let me think about it overnight." And once you have already thought about it overnight, and you look at it and go Mmmmmmmm, you may already say to yourself, "This is the best thing to do right now." It's just a matter of knowing how sequencing time and space structures with tag questions using the question up and command tone down at the right time. Like anything else you've done, when first you thought about it and, yet, weren't sure, once you did it, it was easy after that and you even look forward to doing it again.

It is all in the matter of how you sequence the words. Each word is just a representation for the process to occur.

So think about it and begin to notice where is later, before, now, since when, tomorrow, going to, will, have, and all other temporal predicates. Map out the location and begin to map the locations that other people use, except map them out in your mind. I mean, if you carry a map around to draw on for your clients, I think they'll have some questions. Do it in your mind and you can even gesture with your eyes to verify that you have the information right.

Now when you look at their map, you'll see exactly what they're talking about as they describe their wants, needs, and like-to-haves and everything else they describe. In some places they call easy customers "lay downs." This means that the customer knows just what they want and they're easy to sell to. I think most people who are buying are like that, it's just a matter of recognizing it. Ask someone who knows what they want, ask them what do they need? Then watch them have to switch gears because of the question, when they don't really have to. Why switch tracks when it's unnecessary?

There's a fine line between elicitation and installation so make that distinction for yourself as well as when.

When you're eliciting information, pay attention to *everything* they're doing. If you're not watching what's going on, opportunity will go by . . . somewhere else.

We're going to give you some exercises to flex your linguisticability so you'll recognize which information means what more intuitively. The one thing you can be doing even now, since you know the specifics of your own business, is to design well formed questions that specifically target the information you want or need. Like, when you want to know how much they can spend on their monthly mortgage, for example, ask them how much they can spend on their monthly mortgage, not how are their finances. Ask for the targeted information. The formula is really easy. Write down the information you want, then ask it back in a question. We have people in businesses do this all the time. They design elicitations that are so well targeted that actually are appreciated by their customers because they speed up the process and make it easier for everyone. Make it easy, make it powerful.

When you elicit this information, also listen for and watch what happens to their temporal predicates and their relativity to space. What's in the present, the future, how far into the future? How close to right now?

There are some things that are learned easier unconsciously. Now what I'd like you to do is, I'd like you to try something a little different. Before you look at your client, what I want you to do is to stop, and I want you to just put out in front of you, float up in your mind and look down and see a forty foot puma. Sleek with big white teeth, black fur, shining, and what I want you to do is, in your mind, I want you to float down inside of that Puma. Look out of its eyes. See. And what I want you to do is to put a big mountain on either side of you and be at the beginning of a ravine that goes down and way down that ravine, and look at your client down at the beginning of it. I want you to paw the ground and see them actually lift off of it. I want you to lick your chops and roar for a minute and feel yourself purr, that purr that says, "Your ass is mine."

But I'm not hungry just yet. I want you to look on the mountain on either side of you and see electricity crackin' down that ravine, striking on either side of that client of yours and realize that the lightning is coming from your fingertips. Now, when you look down at that client in your mind, right now, my question is, "Do you feel the same?" The answer most likely is "no", because most of us haven't spent enough time doing what could be ridiculous mental conditioning. However, every neuron inside of you, every fiber in your body, every single cell is affected by your attitude. Your attitude is predictably, by the way, a result of the way in which you view the world. And that's not what you see because your eyes don't really see the world, they compute what's out there. You respond off of planning. If you plan to be a wimp, you will. And many of you have planned that far too well. You know, if you stop and think inside your mind and feel the muscles of a big cat, and realize that . . . what I want you to do is to stalk success. I want you to learn to move one step at a time and look out of the corner of each eye and realize there's opportunity lurking at every corner. If you open up your senses the way cats do, because it's a beautiful thing to watch them move through the night.

I used to work at a night vision lab and we had night vision scopes and I used to love and sit, watch with the scope, and watch a big cat lurk through the night, walking and looking for even the simplest sound. Breathing in and being able to look as only cats can. Where they stop, they're completely silent and their fur begins to float up and when they look at something, . . . they know they can pounce on it, that when the moment is right, they jump right in. They never jump until they know enough to make sure they don't make mistakes. You see, you don't want to be able to rush ahead in the wrong direction, you want to get just enough information to be able to moooooovvvve. Now, put inside your mind the Puma, forty feet high, and while you sleep and dream each night, you move throughout the day you just went through and begin to look at it with new eyes to see, "What did I miss? What more can I learn? How much better can I do this? You begin to hear and see new things in new ways. (Roar) Cause after all, it is your own learning that's important.

Now one of the things we're gonna do is I want you to keep that feeling. You've got your eyes open because there's something more here to learn, but I want you to learn in a new state. I want your eyes to really begin to open up and I want you really to begin to listen.

Now I'll tell you what I want you to do, is I want you to go find yourself someone, stick in a couple new beliefs: "challenge is fun;" "you can sell to anybody." And also sell them the belief that when they go back to where they were, they're gonna make 4 times the amount of money in half the time. No matter what it takes. Get to it.

Well, some of you went inside and you stopped and you asked yourself, "How hard can I make this?" And you were quite successful. But now it's time to just see if we can make this a little easier. Things just don't need to be this hard. We need to find some way of speaking to the part of you that realizes that it just ain't this difficult. "My goodness, gracious", you go, "Well, it must be real complicated cause I don't already know it, and the more you don't know something, the harder it must be. After all, this guy's a doctor or something."

Actually, I'm Dr. Doctor. And the reason I'm Dr. Doctor is

because the Europeans gave me an extra doctorate, they gave me a doctorate of letters. So if any of you have sick letters, I can fix them. I remember I went to the presentation. This was supposed to be like getting an award or an honor or something . . . and I went to this place, and they handed me a pair of tights. And I said "What the hell's this for?" and he says, "Well, we dress up just like we did in the 12th century for graduation." This is from a big university, and these people are getting their doctorates, and I said, "So, when you get all the way through school, they finally dress you up like a fool. Is that what you're saying?" And they said, "Well, no. This is really a great honor." And I said, "So you want me to put on tights, and go out in front of a bunch of people," and I said, "Where I come from, that has a whole different meaning. See when one's from San Francisco, it becomes a lifestyle. I know 'em, a lot of my friends have that lifestyle, if they'd offered them those tights, they'd gone, "Oh blue's just not my color." You know. I'll tell you one of the things that always cracks me up is you know what? To show you how the mind works, I'll always be somewhere in the world and there's a guy who's got two teeth in the front of his mouth and the rest is all space, right? He'll look like he just climbed out of the movie <u>Deliverance</u>, who'll say, "Well, it don't bother me if they want to be homosexuals as long as they don't go after me." Like any decent, self respecting homosexual in an Armani suit, who won't even let a hair be on him is gonna look at this guy and say, "Oh, I want him, yeah!" Now the fact that this guy could even have this question shows me that he has not been to San Francisco and he has not been in the stores, cause he wouldn't go into the Armani store, he'd look in there and say "Oh, there's nothing in there but a bunch of faggots, I wouldn't dare go in there. Next I'd take my clothes off and try sumpin on, why they'd be all over me." I don't think so. Now the fact that he can believe stuff like that means you can get people to believe anything. And that's good if you get to choose.

So I know your unconscious has been close because we've gone through all kinds of things here, some you know about, and some you're gonna learn about tonight. Because, when you go back to wherever it is you're gonna sleep and dream, I want you to consider at the unconscious level, all the things that you've done that were successful without really understanding them.

Cause I know your unconscious has just pulled things out where you've found yourself doing things and you just thought to yourself, you were just in a mood where things began to click and work. You had what's called "good days." Well, it's time for you to begin to grab hold of that feeling, and make yourself believe that every day's gonna start out a good day and get better. That, when you sleep and dream tonight, I want your unconscious to be sorting and searching through your neurosynapsis. Pulling up the best of things and taking the rest of it, and putting it in the same place as old phone numbers and old girlfriends and boyfriends ... in a place where you feel, ooooooooo, "I don't want to do that anymore."

Because the things you do that work are the foundation of your success. And the things you add to it, are what make your success grow. In so far as you can learn to make new tones of voice, use new phrases, get control of your syntax, your body, your movements, see new things, hear new things from the people that you work with, is the range of which you will exceed and excel into the land of greater wealth, greater satisfaction, more sex, more fun every day for the rest of your life. Now I don't know if you're the kind of person that looks forward into your future and sees it as a wonderful thing and feel like you're gonna drool out of the corner of your mouth, you can't wait to get to it. Cause you know you're gonna be able to double the passion with everything in your life; you're gonna be able to look at the most wonderful experience you've had with the person you live with, if you have one, or if not, maybe you'll go get one. Out there there is somebody for everybody and you can take that image in your mind and double and double it again. Never settle for less, and with the person you live with, remember, when you come home, don't be caught up in your day. Stop and take a deep breath and when you open the door, I want you to remember the most wonderful experience you've ever had with them, pull the image closer, make it bigger, make it brighter, crank it way up. So that you can always be more in love and let your imagination run away with you. Now, tonight, while you sleep and you dream, I want your unconscious to sort and search, begin to make changes so that your ears open up 100 times more, your eyes open up and begin to see more. So that when you wake up bright eyed and bushy minded, ready to learn new things. Ready to do new things. I want you to leave any resistance, any case of, as I refer to as, maturity behind. Cause maturity can be a terrible thing if it gets you to reduce your behaviors and not have fun at what you do. We're engaged in one of the most powerful professions on the face of the earth, we get to take people's minds and make them work better. That's what sales people do, you get to get people to make better decisions. People who are negotiators get people to find better solutions, more good for everyone. Cause the trick is to make everything a win/win situation. Rather than cutting up a pie, you make more pies. At one time there was no money, there were no buildings, there were no cars, there were no ideas. And look how many there are now. So basically, it must be possible to make more. Start with making more passion and excitement in your life, open your heart, and the rest will follow. You will find that your flexibility, your ability to do everything, if you make it fun, you'll get a lot more done, a lot quicker, and have time left over to do a lot more of the things in your personal life that you've always wanted to. There's a whole world out there to play with, just waiting for you. Be nice to it.

Remember to use good tonality, and everything else will be easy.

CHAPTER FIVE

MENTAL MAPPING

There's this one place where I go, they made it such as a pleasant place for most people to work that people want to go in there because it's fun. Now there's a notion, how we make things so that what we do is so enjoyable, that we exude pleasure. Because it's when you do that on the telephone, what gets somebody to want to talk to you? Who do you want to talk to on the phone? Cranky people? Who really likes talking to cranky people other than me? Cause I want to see how long they can stay cranky. I also like to be cold calling and you go, "Uh, I have some very bad news." And they go, "Excuse me, who is this?" And I go, "Is this Mrs. So and So?" And they go, "Yeah," and I go, "Well, I'm afraid the price on the sweaters in our store has been lowered, thus removing that profit margin and I just wanted to know if you were interested in coming in." And they go, "They've been lowered?" And I go, "Yeah, it really depresses me. In fact, they've, been cut all the way in half." And they go, "Well, what depresses you?" and I go, "Well it took my commission out of it. But we're gonna raise them back up next week. If you want to wait. And they always go, "Who is this?" I always hear that, "who is this?" And I go, "Just no one, never mind." My favorite phrase: "Never mind." What a great thing. People go, "Well, uh, you know, uh, I have a few questions about this product, process. You know, so you're gonna come into my company and ah, do management training. Uh, what exactly are you gonna do?" And I go, "Never mind about that." Here's another one you have got to keep. This is one of the most powerful phrases in English: "Hold that thought." I love that one. People go, "So, this is really gonna help us?" And I go, "Yeah, hold that thought. For the rest of your life. Now. Let's discuss the terms of this, shall we not? Tag questions. Tag questions allow you to take anybody who has the tendency, cause there are a lot of people who can see how wonderful it is, but they feel they're not ready for it. So, you need to be able to, so to speak, use both sides of human beings because that's the way they make decisions. A lot of human beings make decisions by creating internal conflict. Right. I know you guys don't do that, do you not? Now, what I'd like you to do, is I'd like to try a little mental exercise because I like to try everyday to adjust my attitude so that I can accomplish three things: 1) the reduction of hesitation. It's directly related to insofar as you can reduce hesitation and just try things wantonly, is to the degree you're gonna learn new things.

See, for example, most of you won't walk through the mall, and walk up to people. Somebody picks up a big expensive suitcase, one of those nice Hartman's, or something, that, when you look at the price tag, you go, "Ho!", and you let go of it. What I like to do is walk up to that person and go, "Isn't that a beautiful suitcase? You know, a suitcase like that, can mean you'll have it your whole life. If it even gets a scratch in it, they replace it. It's the most wonderful thing, you know, you could be buying suitcases one a year, two a year, three a year—instead of having something to be proud of that would last your whole life. Do you like things to last?" It's a great gesture to use with men, by the way. It's—they'll all go, "Yes, yes, I do," and you go, "Well, hold on to that thought." And they always go, "Well, how much is that suitcase?" and when I go, "I have no idea I don't work here," they go, "Really?" and they laugh. Salespeople will stand behind me sometimes and when they see that I'm actually selling things, they get angry. I'm just trying to be helpful. They'll go, "What are you doing?" And I'll go, "Well, I was just talking about how wonderful this suitcase is," and they'll literally say to me things like, "Well, stop it." Yeah, that's right you don't want the universe to be on your side.

That's when you turn around and you go, "What did you say your name _was_?" Temporal predicates. This is something else I want you to start listening. Because I'm gonna start using them because people will go, "Oh, man, that's so expensive." And I go, "Yeah, it really was, wasn't it?" Moves it into the past in their mind. And I go, "But if you look at it now, you might begin to see that in relationship to all the qualities it has, it's something you can feel good now about." Now, using language in this way, it's not always quite grammatical, but being able to shift when ideas are, whether they're in the past, whether they're in the future, see I said, "Well, you know, I don't know whether or not," that's an embedded question so they don't really get to answer it. They just get to think of the answer. "I don't know whether or not you can see yourself dressed in your finest clothes, you know, walking into a luxury hotel with this beautiful suitcase, or with a ratty old one with dents in it and stickers all over it. And little tags and tears, and so that people know you're really just a one-time tourist as opposed to an elegant traveler. Which image comes to your mind easiest?"

I don't know about you guys, I travel and it seems like I went in my garage, scary place, your garage, isn't it? It's proof you can sell anything to anybody. Isn't it? How many of you don't have the belief you can sell anything to anybody? Go in your garage and spend a day in there. Worse yet, some of you have what's called a storage unit.

How many of you have to rent an extra garage for extra stuff? I do. I have some — I have one I have no idea what's even it in anymore, it's been too long. Someday, I'm gonna go in there, I'm afraid, though, but when I do, every time I go into one of these things, it's like Christmas, although I've discovered I've bought four more of these since then. That's why I need a storage unit for these, is because I had to make room for the ones I already had.

I recently moved. It was a trick. My teenagers turned of age, you know, 18, and they went away for a few days and so I moved. I thought it was a great idea. I just moved, there's no way I'm gonna fix that place. It's gone, man, it's beat. Having teenagers, because you have one teenager and they travel in packs. They come through and it's been like four years since I've seen the inside of a refrigerator with food in it. You know, they come in like locusts. They land in the house and they eat everything in sight. And, my daughter travels with quite a little band of renegades and they would come into the house. She has friends, my son named one Sasquatch because she would come in—you could tell when she would walk into the kitchen, you could feel the floor "BOOM, BOOM, BOOM" - she'd just take the refrigerator, tilt it up and glub, glub, glub, glub, like that. You know, I'd go to the store, buy $300 worth of food, I'd go out and pick up the mail and come back and there wouldn't be anything but bones on the counter. And the dog would look at me, point over, and the kibble was gone, too.

Actually, I'd bought these little dog burger things because my dog is small and I bought these little dog burger things, and they were in a box, and the box got wet so I took them out and I stuck 'em in the refrigerator. It seemed like the thing to do. Right? Well, I discovered the kids really like these things. And they're not that expensive, right? And it seems to fill them up a lot because I guess they have a lot of bone marrow and stuff in there. So I started buying 'em and putting 'em in plastic bags and putting 'em in the refrigerator, and when, one day, my daughter was in there and she was frying one up, actually she was frying three up, one for her and two for her friends, Sasquatch, you know, and they had the buns out and they were putting stuff on there, and I walked in and I said, "Are you making hamburgers?" and I looked in the pan and I said, "Oh, if you were making hamburgers I was gonna have one." And they looked at me and I said, "That's dog food." And they looked at me, checked it out, and they said, "You're such a liar, you're always saying that, get out of here." And I said, "Okay, never mind. So this is what you want to eat?" and she said, "Just get out, out out out."

Of course I moved. I was tired of eating doggy burgers. Actually, they wouldn't even leave the doggy burgers in there. I get this kind of stuff a lot because since my dog's small, just as a ritual, sometimes I like to heat the dog's food up, you know, because you can con them into eating stuff easier that way. You know, you can just take the dog food, throw it in a pan, with a little water, you can put a little garlic powder on it, you know, a little salt and pepper, and the dog goes, "Hey, it's human food. Give me that. I don't want the dog food. I'll take that stuff, the stuff with the garlic powder on it, yeah, yeah, the stuff like you make for yourself." And I go, "Oh, no, you can't have this, get away." You know, you have to play these games, because dogs are pretty smart, you know. Humans, you can just go, eat it, yum, but you tell the dog to eat it, it looks up at you and goes, "(sniff, sniff, sniff) . . . I want what you have." Because especially if you serve food when you're eating, you know, the dog goes (sniff, sniff) he goes, "This is much better." But if you put garlic powder on it, you can fool them, you know. That's because I put a lot of garlic on everything. You have to when you have teenagers, because the only stuff left in the refrigerator looks more like a biology project than anything else. I don't know what the other thing is. There's some genetic phenomenon with teenagers, where a half inch of milk always gets left in the carton. You ever notice that? Just that much. And orange juice, too. There's always that much, so that they don't have to have the responsibility of taking the carton and putting it in the garbage. And mine, the garbage thing is right next to the refrigerator because, usually when I get there there's just bones and wrappers and I like to have it be close.

That's what happens. There you are, your teenagers, they were so nice and so cute when they were small and then they come and take all of your money and your car. Right? I even had three cars, two teenagers. I'd get up and there wouldn't be one. Figure that out. They'll loan one of your cars to their friends. You'll get up in the morning, have nothing to drive, nothing to eat and no money. You do that for a couple of years, things get tense, plus, there's this genetic thing where they can make nonverbal signals that make you go insane inside your head. They go, "ble-hhh," and suddenly your body goes (wkejejrjerjzzzzz) and you hear yourself saying stuff your parents said to you. It's really frightening, it's what told me anchoring works. And then there's my daughter, who taught me arm levitation. Where I could reach back and grab a hold of my wallet, let it float involuntarily out. You know. It's like I'd see the money disappear and I'd say, "What am I doing? I must be in a trance," you know, the extraction trance. That's the same one I induce other people in and I come home and they can take it from me. I'm just an intermediary between my daughter, my dog and the world. Think about it. Now I know probably some of you are laughing because this is so true.

But just think that it's your job to go back and help others. Like they have dogs, cats and children, too.

Now, remember I want you to begin to make changes so that your ears open up 100 times more, your eyes open up and begin to see more. Start with making more passion and excitement in your life, open your heart, and the rest will follow. Make it fun, you'll get a lot more done, a lot quicker, and remember to use good tonality, and everything else will be easy.

There's a list of something that seems to me to be a synopsis of most sales forces. And I talked about needing a road map, that there are certain things that most people don't pay attention to, when they're in the activity of engineering influence.

One is that you can't do it if you don't have their attention. You skip over that phase. And when I say attention, I mean their full attention. I've seen too many times, and too many situations, people start babbling away to somebody who is staring at something, who is not listening. And, when you do that, you're not able to influence them, especially at the unconscious level. I think of sales, I think of negotiation as a by product of skills of the hypnotists. And if you don't think of it that way, you'll discover that you make a lot less money, so for those of you who are interested in making less money, keep it up. For those who are not, then the thing to do is to realize that when you get somebody's attention, that it's okay to let them just stare at something and wait, until you have them.

Because any form you can get their attention in is fine. I tried something. These guys that worked in this car lot there, that had worked there for years in their seats, and they had a job much like the people at Xerox. The people at Xerox, what they had to do in order to sell something was to lift the phone, for years. All they had to do was pick up the phone and go, "Okay, you want five." They'd pick up the phone again, and go, "Oh, yes, okay, you'd like 10." Because, there was the only Xerox machine, their copier was the largest selling product in the history of the US.

Interestingly enough, when the gentleman developed it, it took him 15 years to get somebody to finance mass marketing it because of the following comment, "Well, if people want to copy, they'll just use carbon paper." Really, do you know how many people probably went out and shot themselves when those things hit the market? People consumed them like wild fire. Now what happened was, at a certain point in time Xerox lost its exclusivity over the technology.

Finally, the patent ran out and every Japanese company on the face of the earth made a copier. And the guys at Xerox were sitting in their offices, staring at the phone, and it wasn't ringing. And it wasn't going to ring. Now, one of the things that happened is that Xerox then went out and spent a fortune, and I mean a fortune, getting some of the most "brilliant," here was the problem, psychologists on the face of the earth. These are people who've never sold anything in their lives. They, then, designed a big sales course. Now, I attended that course, and many others. I went around, you see, I wanted to find out what people knew about. There was nothing inside of the entire course, which by the way started off with a one-day, then they had a three day, then they had a week, then they had month. Special training, if you were gonna get really advanced. In all the courses there was not one thing about *listening*. There was not one thing that told you anything that you could actually do. There wasn't anything to give you, anyway, which is the third tier of what I want to know, when you had done anything, either.

There were ways of evaluating a person's personality, as if, by the time somebody walks in a room, and looks at copy machines up there, you're gonna be able to influence them, or go into a store and sell them your copiers versus others, or a business. Because at this time, businesses were being deluged with these personality things.

I had this consulting company once and there was this receptionist there. And this client came up and, you know, when you have clients like we had, you had to be real careful and the guy came up and had no appointment, and had a big bag of literature under his arm. That's always how you tell a nut, by the way. They have a lot of writing with them cause no one wants to listen to them. He came up to the door and said, "I'm here to see Bandler and I'm not leaving until I do." And he sat down, in the reception area and everybody that came by, he was looking at them with wild eyes and writing madly and finally spread stuff on the floor and she asked some of the other people I had working there to help because they'd all come in and they would look at this stuff, and she would ask them, "Say, can you handle this?" And they would go, "I'm busy right now," and go in the other room." My office, by the way, wasn't in the same building. I found if it was, they'd pester me all the time. So I had one up the street with video cameras in the building, and I used to just sit up there and watch them all. It was great. So I'd been watching this all morning long because I was fascinated with this. I thought this was good.

Well, this lady decided that somebody has to deal with this guy, so she told him, she said, "Gather up your things and follow me." And she took him into the back, and all the way back in and into the office of the person who at that time was running that particular division of the company, had him set all his stuff down, because they had an office big enough to spread it out on the floors, and left him there alone. Now I'm watching on the video cameras, and as soon as the door closes, I mean it was like lightning, this guy was in the filing cabinets. He pulled out the cases of all the clients that we'd had for years. And then he noticed a big knife and picked it up.

Well, the guy turned around and there was a big mirror in the room. And I don't know if he was trying to decide whether to kill himself or one of us, but it seemed to me that when you have an estranged, wild human being, the thing that you don't do, especially one who doesn't have an appointment, isn't really your client, the thing you don't do is arm them. It's not like step #1, with clients, arm them. Step #2, bear your chest. I used the primitive approach. I called a friend of mine at the Santa Cruz police department and the guy came down and I gave him the keys to the back door to that office and he went up by the door and knocked on it, and then I, told him, I said, "All you have to do is tap on the door, and then step aside and then tap on the door, and go, 'Olly, Olly, Oxen Free.'" And the guy opened the door, actually it was nice he put the knife down first. He opened the door, I was watching on the cameras because I sure as hell wasn't going down there. I've seen these people before, you know. It's fine when they're locked up or chained down or something. But when they're armed, you want somebody else who is armed. They pulled this guy off, handcuffed him, and while they were dragging him away, he's waving his hands around wildly, even though he was cuffed. They finally had to cuff him hand and toe, and drag him away. They brought him down, booked him and then in the interest of justice, of course, the courts arraigned him and OR'd him in less than an hour. And, in an hour and 15 minutes, he was back. Now, she decided, well, obviously the police aren't gonna help, so, what she did is she started calling the other people that she thought were just as nutty and having them come down, too. We were gonna have a convention. I don't know where this idea came from, I mean what could she have been thinking, because I had a file called nuts.

And these were the people that I just didn't want to deal with because, they weren't there to get help, they were there, because they wanted us to join in what conspiratorial phenomenon was going on in their mind. For example, there was one person who was convinced that, actually, I was not from this planet, and that all this Neuro-Linguistic Programming — was a way of programming the whole world to enslave it. And the first time he showed up he showed up with a big shot gun. And that's, by the way, why I had my office down the street. He kicked in the front door, he's got the shotgun, and went, "We must all kill him. We have to overthrow him," and began unloading rounds in the building. That time she called the police right away, but now she called him back. The idea is to get rid of people like this primarily because they don't have any money. You know, if you're gonna see them, I want to see them in a safe environment. I want to go into a nice mental hospital where I can scare the hell out of them. Not the other way around. Now, the other thing that she did is she did something, that I thought was interesting. I told her, "I want to have a representative from one of these copier companies come in here." She popped open the phone book and called every single one of them. And gave them all the same appointment. She buzzed me, and she said, "Can you see them at 11?" And I said, "Sure." And I said, "What company are they from?" And she said, "Copying company." I said, "Okay." Suddenly there's this entourage, because I had a big iron gate in front of my office, and I heard (thirp, thirp) and I turned on the cameras and here out in front are these human beings. And they all had brief cases, and a wild look in their eye. And I thought, "Oh, this is gonna be good. Nuts, again." So I buzz and I said, "What do you want?" And they all started waving brochures in the air. So I let them into the lobby, I made them all sit down and I said, "Who the hell are you people?" One guy was from Xerox, he was the one that barely breathed. He sat there like he was depressed. Because after all he learned selling the psychological approach. And then there were all these other guys.

There were guys who knew nothing about copy machines, but boy they knew how to sell and they knew, in a crowd, he who squeaks the most gets the oil. And there was one guy, who is just screaming. Finally, one guy out of all of them does something unusual, because they were all trying to talk at the same time, and I told them to shut up and I asked them, "Why are you all here?" and they said, "Well, because you need a copy machine." And I said, "Well, what did we do, run off copies of the salesman, what's the story here?" And this one guy, just sat there, casually unbuttoned his shirt, took it off, unbuttoned his pants and walked over in his shorts. "I'm trying to get your attention." And I said, "You got it. Almost got it anyway." Well, I figured somebody who was enthusiastic . . . Now, I actually got a copy machine from this guy because I liked his style. Out of 17 guys there, all there with their briefcases, massive brochures, shuffling through their brochures and stuff. Most of them were more interested in the brochures than they were in me. This guy didn't have anything with him. He said, "It's in the car." He said, "Let's go to lunch, it's too crowded here." I like that, I thought that was good. Suddenly an idea dawned on my mind. I decided that, for my little hobby that I did a couple days a week, I would try some things that were out of the ordinary, to see if I could get some attention. Because after all, this is not a good time to be selling cars.

By the way, even though I'd gathered up some people from the country club and the Toyota lot, which was across the street. They didn't like me much. I tried things like I went out and I got myself one of those little yellow jackets, like the guys that worked on the roads do. One of those little stop signs. "Slow." And I went out and I'd stand on the road with the sign and wave them down. Especially if I saw a Volvo. Because at the time, that's when Volvo was going through the law suits about being lemons. And, there was a lot of truth to that. I had a friend, who had at the time a

Volvo, and even the glove box didn't work on this thing. It was that, the Jaguars, too. You could always just walk up to anybody, anywhere in town as they were getting into a Jaguar and just look at them and go, "How depressing," and they'd go, "What?" And I'd go, "You must spend a lot of time in the shop." And they'd go, "Yeah," and I'd go, "Doesn't it grate on you?" He'd be down there in moments, and I'd just go up there — there's a parking lot about three blocks up — and I'd walk up and it seemed like that's where the cars were. I'd go and see who looked at their car, and when they looked at it like they wanted to have it out with it. Then I got another idea. I thought, "Gee, who do people really trust?" because for me always in the second stage and all of these kinds of sales things. It says establish rapport. I thought, "Uuuuum," Because, once you have somebody's attention you should be able, without being a rocket scientist, to know if you have their full attention. The trick is to notice if you are more concerned over your brochures or this or that.

I recently decided I wanted to buy a four wheel drive vehicle. So what I did is, in my ignorant way of doing things, I went out and rented each one for a week, until I decided which one I liked. I went down to the dealership, and this is an unusual opening line, I walked in through the door, looked at the one I wanted, the salesman walked over to me and said, "Excuse me, what are you doing here?" And I looked at him and said, "I'm after your job." And he said, "What?" And I said, "Where's your boss?" And he said, "Well he's back there behind the window." I said, "Wait here." And I went in and then his boss came out and fired him. Smart guy, because this guy's idea of establishing getting your attention was to piss you off. Now, I don't recommend that that's the way that you go about it, because when you piss people off and attach it to you, it doesn't work well. However, if you piss them off and aim it in the right direction it can be useful.

Now one of the things, that I want to teach you is a little trick, that I've learned through the years as I went through any kind of a sales pitch, whatsoever, and I started to get some flak from them, that when I could tell things weren't going good. It didn't matter, whatever it was. I always would get out of my chair and I would turn around and I'd say, "Now that's what you normally hear from a salesman." and I'd go, "that kind of activity." And I'd point back towards the chair, "It's that kind of shit that really annoys you, isn't it?"

People go, "Yeah. It is." And I'd turn around and I'd go, "Now, the other companies around here, that sell cars, you've probably been to a few of them, think about them. That's the kind of thing you're gonna get there." Because any time you get a negative response like that, you want to make sure you drop back and immediately disassociate it from you and associate it with something else. I picked the Toyota lot because there was a big window there. And I actually got people so pissed off now and then, that when people would leave they'd stop over there and yell at people. I do like doing things. They'd go across the street and they'd walk up to one of the guys and flip them the bird. And they'd walk away. And all the guys in the Toyota lot would look at each other, and they'd look in the window over there. And they'd go, "What the hell do they tell people?" I even had one guy walk over and he walked in and he said, "What the hell are you telling people about us?" he said, "This guy just came over there and cussed me out." And I said, "The truth. You were trying to kill their children." And they'd go, "I didn't try and kill anybody's children." And I said, "You try and sell those collapsible cars, don't you?"

Now at that time I want to tell you, because I know somebody that had a Toyota Corolla, and it was parked by the side of the road, and next to the road there was a small embankment that went down about ten feet, and then there was a driveway which had come off on an angle. The ground was a little wet, the tires sank down and the car rolled slowly down and landed on the driveway, and was totaled. Flattened like a pancake. I know, it was my car. Somebody gave it to me, when they went to Europe, to drive. When they came back, they weren't happy. Now when I saw a car crush like that, suddenly, what dawned in my mind, most people would've said, "Oh, I crushed my friend's car," I thought to myself, "I could use this as a selling technique." So I had the car delivered down and we put it outside in front of our place. A flattened crushed Toyota Corolla and I went down to the theatrical supply house and got myself a mannequin, some blood paint and put it inside with an arm sticking out. And then I got two small dolls from a toy store all right and had them laying out and a little sign that said, "Think about it. Is it worth it?" The Toyota people hated that. Because anybody that was going into the Toyota lot, when they turned around they'd look and see us over there and there it was, with the arms hanging out and everything and on the side it said, "Get your hands on a Toyota," which was their slogan at the time. Now, I want to tell you that the guy that owned the Toyota lot just got into it with the guy that owned the place that I was volunteering my time to. They actually had such a big fight about it, that they made me remove it. But I just thought it was just kind of a flexis billboard. The flexis art is living art, it's where life becomes art. And to me, I always figured the best form of advertisement is any flexis art you can create, that it builds in its own message. That I know, for example, here are things that strike me as not good business. For example, the guy that owned the Toyota lot, drove a Mercedes. That's a gift from the gods.

You film that and show it in your show room. I mean, to me, this is good advertisement. This is where life imitates itself. If he's afraid to drive one, how come he's willing to sell one to you, because he hates you? That's why they go over there and get mad. I go, "He's willing to have your children die, while he feeds off them. He laughs at people like you." I've gotten people so pissed off, they went over in force sometimes. They moved the Toyota lot across town. I'm not kidding. He said he was planning to get a new, bigger place because they were doing so well. Or at least had been.

Now, when I set the idea of competition . . . to me, because I don't think there is a limit to the amount of things to go around. I know that when they put a whole bunch of car lots in one place, they all sell more cars than when they've put one out in the mid-dle of nowhere. That your ability to realize that you know there is no limit in the number of things, but when it comes down to pure competition . . .

To me I view it as fun. Other people view it as stress. From the standpoint of stress, you can't do business. To me, I view clients as food, because that's what they are. When they come in to buy something, when it's the matter of who is going to get this money, it's different than "is it possible?" Because, for me, I was selling cars to people who weren't planning to buy one. Most of the time I'd drive down and I'd go, "Now, where would be a good place to sell cars?" And I'd go, "Repair places."

Find people who are frustrated out of their mind and tell them they can dump more money into this hunk of junk, or they could feel wonderful. Do you want to feel wonderful or do you want to feel bad? Think about it. Now most of them didn't say to me, "Well I really want to feel bad." Actually I would've had a ten-dency to amplify their bad feelings. Nothing personal. But I found that if I turned them up just enough . . . because I like to ask things like, "I wonder if you can imagine what will break next?"

I went down to a place that specialized in foreign cars one

evening and for a small price and a few cocktails, I managed to get the guy to go through and give me all of the repair reports on Volvos and Jaguars and a few other cars; big giant receipts and just on one car, where it was just one right after the other after the other. And I xeroxed those files so that I could walk up to people and I'd go, "Is this your Volvo?" And they'd go, "Yeah." And I'd go, "How old is it?" And they'd go, "Well you know, it's two, three years old." And I go, "Oh, it's just about to start." And they go, "What?" And I go, "Well, have you had any repairs recently?" And I said, "I'd like to show you what's going to happen. I'd like you to know what your future is going to be like." And I'd show him the file. Some of these cars, it was unbelievable. . . there was one that spent over 200 days in the repair shop. Think about it . . . 200 days . . . that's like, you get to visit your car on weekends. I know. I had a Jaguar and I actually got to the point where it was either me or the car, one or the other. I didn't even sell it. And I got the personal satisfaction of burning it. I did. Drove it off a cliff and burned it. I decided no car would ever make me feel that way again, It wasn't about money anymore, it was personal. I know that the car did it to me because it wanted to because it wouldn't break down. When I'd leave, it would always break down half way there. Not only that, but it would do it in the most demeaning of ways. It would do it in a place where you couldn't pull over. It would do it in a place where I knew it was a personal thing.

Now the other sales people that were down at this place told me the kinds of things that I was doing were not professional. And I said, "Quite to the contrary," I said, "Anybody that doesn't vary their behavior to find out how to generate more business and find out what they do is not going to do well, they'll be like you." Now while I am down there, because, of course, the guy that owned the place is not going to get rid of me at this point because I am the only one selling anything, right? And that's because I will go to just about any limit just to find out what will work.

Well when I was down at the costume store, bringing back the stuff after they made me remove the Toyota, there it was in radiant luxury, just sitting out there on the stand. It came to me all at once: "establish rapport." There was a catholic priest outfit and I thought, "Trust, it's built in." What could be better? "Bless you, my children, for you need a car." Now, I never told anyone I was a catholic priest, I just put it on. And then I'd walk up to people and I'd go, "Me lassie, you seem to be having a wee bit of trouble with the car." That's when it went wild. I said, "Just tell me your troubles." "Ah I can't afford big payments." "Well, we'll work it out for you. I'm sure we'll find some way. You know, I've got a friend down here, who will take care of you." And you know, I've never had anybody ask even after we went down and I showed them the car. I gave them a good price, gave them a good deal, right? Set them up and I would send them in the other room and they'd sign them up on paper. They would always come out and go, "Thank you, father." And I'd go, "It's all right, me lassie, don't you worry. If you have any problems you bring it back right here." You know what? I thought the guys that worked at this place were going to flip because they knew I was Jewish.

And the one guy told me that it was a sacrilege and I said, "It's a costume, for Christ's sake." I said, "Everybody rents them," I said, "except these guys rent these costumes at Halloween." So I went back to the costume store and started going, "What else? Can I see that policeman's uniform there?" Maybe we'll try . . . oooooh, look at that there, I'll try one of those." Because what I wanted to do, was for me, I was just trying to learn to find out what lengths you could go to. I mean, to me, if you don't vary your behavior, you don't try things, you don't find out what will work.

I tried things. For example, I tried stand up in a night club because the band took a break and I just walked up to the microphone and I said, "I know that you are all here for the meeting, and I want to know how many of you are just sick and tired of the gas prices thing?" And everybody goes, "Yeah." I said, "How many of you just really want to get a good car anyway?" People would go, "Yeah," and I said, "Well, those of you who are interested I want you to see me in the back."

I picked up fifteen people in one night. I just went there to have drinks. The guy asked me to come in and play for a few tunes that night with him, an old friend. He said, "I know that you don't play much, why don't you get down and play a few songs." I played a few songs and sold fifteen cars. They had to come down the next day and picked up their Cadillacs. I only brought pictures with me. I had names for the cars, too. I found out that was the easiest way to sell a used car, is to have a name for it. You personalize things, right? You know, I'd show them and I'd say, "See this Lincoln? This is Barbara." And I'd go, "I like Barbara." You'd be surprised, you know, ten o'clock, eleven o'clock at night in a cocktail lounge, you could sell just about anything.

One time, the high way patrolman, who was a friend of mine, was doing a thing inside the schools and I, at the time, was doing a project. I took all the educationally handicapped children, because I have a personal pet peeve about this stuff. And I took all of them in one school for one week and moved them to the top of their class. This pissed the teachers off because they would give them tests like the others, and they had their bright little bright kids, and I went around and screwed them all up. I did that at recess, it was easy. It's really not that hard, you know. You just walk up to them, lift their arm up and tell them to close their eyes and say, "The next time you get a spelling test you won't be able to make images. You'll just sound everything out." They did that to some of you, didn't they?

Those of us that learned to spell phonically, and you know, I love that, when you go up and ask how to spell a word, and they tell you to look it up in a dictionary. If I knew how to spell it, I wouldn't need a damned dictionary. And they made it sound all so important, and how many of you now have a button on your computer that you can press? Take your mouse and go "spelling" and bam! it's over. Except that if you spell it like another word the computer will go, "oh that's fine" and then in one of those sentences I walked down the street Fine, it was fine. Well that's because computers can't make the distinction. Your mistake must be gross or not at all. So those of you who spell pretty well actually have more trouble using the spelling program because you will misspell and it will be spelled like another word. Those of us that learned how to spell phonetically can use these computers because when we do it, most of the time, the computer goes, "I'll be damned if I know what that is. Can you try another version for me?"

Now, the thing that happened with the high way patrol, which I thought was beautiful, is that, here I am working with these kids. They came down and they asked me, they said, because I'd had some interaction with the police and they also knew that I drank, and that I was good at it. I'm one of the few people that actually smuggled a bottle of vodka into jail. I went to visit somebody, we were working on a legal case and I asked the guy, "Can I bring you anything?" And he said, "Yeah," he said, "Bring me a bottle of vodka." So I did. And they never did figure out where I hid the bottle of vodka, because before we went in, I was working with the lawyer. They searched us, they searched everything, and when they found the empty bottle of vodka in there and him singing away, it wasn't very discrete. I thought he was going to use it over a period of time. I didn't know he was going to drink it all at once. But, they asked me, they said, "You know, you got patted down. You weren't carrying anything with you. Where did you hide the bottle of vodka?" And I said, "In my hands." And they said, "That's absolutely impossible." And I said, "No, it's not." The next time I went there, when I left he had another bottle of vodka. Now, it was so easy. All I did was took cardboard and made it look like a thermos. It even had a top that you could take off.

That I'd taken off another thermos, and had hot coffee in it. They'd open it up and there was hot coffee and it was only this big. And I put plaster of paris and a bottle of vodka underneath it. Smuggling seemed like a challenge to me. I modeled those guys with the CIA, too. But, it was real interesting working with those people because I got to ask them all kinds of questions and stuff. They have, by the way a rather interesting sales program: "Do what we want or we'll kill you." Um, which works for me. I become very flexible. I mean just tell me what you want. And they go, "We can't. It's a secret, now give it to us."

I want to begin to train your eyes. To begin to notice things. One way is, I'm going to ask you, whatever it is that you sell, and if you don't sell anything, make something up . . . I'm going to ask you to go into the phase where you start to notice the sign posts that tell you when you have somebody's attention and the question is, when have you? . . . because I like to ask them questions. I've always told people that I was a decision engineer because, if you said you were a sales person, it's a negative anchor. And you say, "Oh yeah, there's plenty of sales people around here," I said, "You can see them sitting over there in their suits. You know what they'll try to do to you." And they go, "Yeah, I know what you mean." I go, "Well, I'm the decision engineer here. See, I'm only here to find out how you make good decisions." Now begin to ask them questions about the difference between the good decision and a bad decision. But while you are doing this I want you to breathe at the same rate they are breathing. I want you to talk in roughly the same rate that they do, and if they are using a lot of visual words, use a lot of visual words.

But this is the most important thing. As you start to do this, I want you to shift and begin to speak at the rate that they are breathing. You can feel that hit you like a drum can't you? Even a few seconds of it like that, and something inside you goes, "Wow! Yeah, right." Because contrary to popular belief, people like to be influenced, if you do it well. Think about it. When somebody seduces you, they're influencing you. And if they do it well, it feels good, doesn't it? Now, if they do it badly, it feels like shit, right. For example, last night, out of my hotel room window, their was a bunch of guys standing on the corner and every time a car would drive by with a woman in it, they'd go, "yo baby." Now do they really think that that's going to work? I don't think so, for some reason. I can't see women going, "Oh, put the brakes on, man." Then there were guys driving by in cars doing the same thing, yelling at the women that were walking down the street. Like you know, the woman's going to take out a grappling hook and get that bumper and slow them down.

See the trick is to notice that you are going to get a positive state. The problem is, you can't get one if you are not in one. I see people and they drive down the freeway, and it stresses them out. Me, I look at all the buildings full of money, going, "It will be mine." See, you need to be able to go inside and make sure that your tonality is pleasant and that you access wonderful states and then, when you mirror somebody and you begin to speak at the rate that they are breathing, then they are going to start feeling better than they've felt before. They are going to go, "I'm starting to feel good."

Because at that moment in time, I'm going to ask you to do something, which is, I want you to begin to mirror them, you're already breathing at the same rate. But what I do is I just start smiling and if they smile, like you . . . As a matter of fact, you know, I still have a Lincoln and I know you've been thinking about it, ever since I started talking about it. I mean it's got those big leather seats, and I love those buttons to roll down the window and you know, I put a big cattle horn on the front of mine. A six cattle horn that says get out of my way or your screwed. Never mind. You wouldn't want to keep that powerful state, would you? "Come to me Barbara, come to me." I want to introduce you to Barbara. She will change your life.

It's just something about those big Lincoln's, you know. People go, "Why do people buy those big gas guzzlers?" Because they weren't driving, that's why. I didn't drive very far. I drove thirteen miles to work and thirteen miles back and every once in a while I stopped at a bar. Stopping doesn't use any gas at all. I found that the more I was stopped the less gas I used. It always amazes me, when people are stuck in traffic, bumper to bumper, they let their engines run. Not me, I turn mine off and get out of the car and go knock on people's windows. Start passing out literature. It's like that thing about that airline where they strap them down, I think that's great. I walk up and down and I look and I go, "They're all strapped down. This is great! Good! Break out the product . . . we've got them." You just go and hand shake interrupt with each one of them. They are just sitting there on the plane.

Now, what I want you do is to start playing with this, because what you are after, is looking. The goal of this exercise, that you are about to do, is to look. Oh yeah, there's an exercise here. I'm going to teach you, by the way later on, the contract interrupt technique. It's much like a hypnotic technique that was used by Milton. He did something called the hand shake interrupt to get people into trance. I do the contract interrupt. I usually like to start out my sales pitches by having them sign the contract and then I do the sales pitch. I find it works much easier that way. And the look of fear on their face. They've already signed it, but they don't know why. But I have it in my hand and then what I do is, I slowly start to rip it up as I convince them, that they want it. It's an interesting polarity. I don't actually rip it up, just that carbon stuff around the edge. But its a way of being able to induce a state, by which you can get people to act as if the contract is for service of the product. And so you can tell whether or not you will ever get any buyer's remorse. It's a test.

Because to me, I just blatantly get people's attention. Then what I do. I find a way of knowing if I have rapport. This is the important point about having a road map that tells you where you are. I know when I have their attention by the look on their face. That's one way to know.

For example, the zipper technique. You ask yourself, "What is the zipper technique?" Let your imagination run wild and you'll have one, too. This is what I am after, your ability to begin to think of, "What can I do?" Because, if you are in a situation and you're not getting someone's attention, the term is "escalate." Now, there's the heart attack technique. That one works really good. That's where you keep a little thing with pills in your shirt pocket. You just need candy ones, you don't need real pills, and some of you've done this, haven't you? And then I used this in the furniture store, because people walk too fast in furniture, like they are looking for a specific couch. Right? Like, you can't make them look at another one. Or you can't change the fabric and they zoom back and forth. But you are going to have the exact one sitting out and as they walk by, you suddenly go, "Uh uyh uh arrrrgh." You know, if they save your life they have to buy something from you. I don't know why, but they do. It's some unwritten law.

Now, about the exercise. The exercise is simply to start to pitch somebody on something but to concentrate yourself on making sure you follow the following rules: Do not know what you are going to say before you say it; so that you hear your voice coming out of your mouth. Remember you can always change it. And I want you to ask questions. And the kind of questions I want you to ask, first are the ones that get people to ramble. I want you to see if you can throw in at least three rhetorical questions by which you would get a yes. You know, you do want to be happy, don't you? And they go, "Yeah." And you go, "Well, you want to enjoy your life and you know, that if you buy just the right thing and make just the right decision, then you'll enjoy yourself, won't you?" Tag questions are always the way of getting a good rhetorical response. And I realize I'm asking you to do a number of things at the same time, but that's because, if you can't, you ought to go out and get a real job, like being a social worker. Something where you don't need skills. Something where, your tenure of being a school teacher . . . They do this in the US: if you can work somewhere for three years you have a job for life. But you know, the quality of the education in the US is directly disproportionate to the fact that school teachers don't have to get any better at what they do, right? They don't have to produce results. On the other hand, those of us who are engaged in business, who are engineering influence, we are directly rewarded in relationship to the competency with which . . . Wouldn't it be neat if doctors got paid that way? It's like you had to pay them as long as you were healthy.

Now, what I want you to do, is to throw in a few of these things. But primarily while all of this is going on, I want you to focus on your breathing just like I've been doing here. So the minute I smile, you have to smile and then when I nod, you have to nod, don't you? So that, even though they know that you're in total control with their physiology it feels so good, they like it. Now, an important part of this is that, while you are doing it, you constantly, yourself, go into pleasant states. I'm thinking of all the girls I dated when I was 20 years old. They were great, weren't they? Now, as soon as you can get a non verbal response, it goes pace pace lead. But while I am going through and I'm starting to do things like listen to what predicates are used, whether he thinks of pictures or words, it's this non verbal part that I want you to concentrate on. Because as soon as you can control the tempo of your voice so that it matches their breathing . . . Somebody asked me yesterday. They came up to me, and they said, I can't see people's breathing. And I asked, "Where are you looking?" And they said, "Well I'm looking at their mouth." And I said, "Well, you can't see it there. It's not like it comes out colored, you know. You have to look at the chest. And watch the breathing down here." And if they don't, because some people just don't breath much, then what you have to do is get them to breath a little more. Until you juice them, they won't. So you begin to set the pace, your language. Take a deep breath and they will, too.

Somebody said, "What does all this have to do with free will?" And I said, "There isn't anything that is free, is there? Because after all, you wouldn't want something second rate, would you?" Isn't that a great question? You hate it when things break, don't you? You'd rather feel good, wouldn't you?

Now this is what I want, I want it so that when you stop, they stop to the point where you begin to feel that you can get non verbal gestures, and this kind of stuff here. You know, smiles and things. You can even throw in other stuff, you know. Start from scratch, nobody knows (Richard scratches his nose). But they might find it **handy** and **uplifting**. See there are whole levels at which you can do this and the trick is that you are always going to want to weave these levels together. You're going to want to put language patterns in. I love it when they fight it, too. Remember the rule of thumb: when in doubt, escalate. Savor the unexpected. Why not be blatant about it? I believe that your unconscious can do anything. I've said, "You know, if you make part of your life more sumptuous, why wouldn't the rest of it get that way?"

I mean, think about it. If you could wait in line at the bank, because these are the worst salespeople in the world, you know . . . banks now have to sell. It's so funny. I love this. Banks have never had to be nice to you and now, there are so many of them, they actually are ordering, we just got paid three and a half million dollars to go in and train, in just one county in California, people who worked at this bank, how to go this far to be nice to the customers. Just enough rapport skills, no matching predicates, none of this. Just using good tonality and trying to speak at the same rate as people. Right. And noticing whether or not they were smiling. Because this raised the assets of this particular bank, by one billion dollars in less than a year and that's all we taught them.

Well think of it. It's such a novel idea. Somebody is being nice to you in the bank. Do they do that where you go? It's so you'll come in to begin with and they'll take your money, but they are real shits about giving it back. We have these ATM cards, right? I have $20,000 in my account but they will only give me $300. What the hell is that about, it's my money. They go, "Well, we are just trying to protect you." And they go, "Why would you want more cash than that after dark? Just what do you plan to do?" "I plan to buy a car and a plane ticket and a house and I want to pay cash for it, it should be my right. We are supposed to live in free societies, but thanks for telling us how to bank." "I'm sorry, you'll have to line up over here." I don't think so. You know, I see those lines, and something inside of me goes "fiott

fiott," it goes, "Wait a minute, this is my money, I don't have to wait in line. Just because they've put a velvet rope up doesn't mean I have to go Mooo, Mooooo." Because it's always a good chance they've made these places like churches for a reason, so that when you walk in they make you feel small and helpless and be on your best behavior one day a week.

Okay what I want you to do is I want you to do this with someone else and have somebody else observe to find out if the person is doing this right and then make a few suggestions, kind of change each other a little bit. Take the time to see if you can kind of polish yourselves up a little bit. Take about just five, ten minutes and do it. Go for it.

By the way, when you are selling things. Age regression is very powerful, and not in techniques. You always want to induce that part of people that's a wanting consumer, known as a teenager. Somebody was just telling me recently about the methods that their son uses to get them to buy Nintendo, and Sega games and to rent them, because it saves them money, because they don't have to buy them. I think that's one of the interesting things, that, what people won't buy for themselves, they'll buy for other people. There are many people inside of their strategies, that if it's just for them, that's when you say, well, I actually heard somebody in here, I like this one. This is a great line, it goes, "But don't you want a diamond?" It's, "Wouldn't you like to have a diamond? It would be such a shame that you had to wait until you were so old you couldn't appreciate it." Yes, write that one down. I spend a lot of time in jewelry stores and those of you who have seen my wife know why. My wife owns a jewelry company. I figured, "What the hell, we might as well." We had enough stock. And she deals in rare gems and antique jewelry and stuff and so, she buys it, I sell it. And I found that it's so easy to prospect in that business, all you have to do is go to the opera. It's great. You go down to the opera house, it doesn't matter what's going on. I found that, with any product, the best place is to go where they use it. If you sell coffee machines, I'd be standing outside of Kinko's all day long. The idea that there are some people that think they are glued to where they were. And it's not the case. Now somebody asked me, "What about this limited channel communication stuff?" Okay, how do you hear, how do you know because see, if you are on the telephone, how do you know what somebody's breathing is? It's actually the easiest, you can hear them. If you can't hear people breath on the phone get a better phone, or better ears. One or the other. Because when you are talking to people on the phone, you can hear them breath. And also, when they are talking to you, you can find out how long it is, between each breath.

Now, as I listen to people, as I walk through the training room, I notice that some of you used the coffee technique, to control your tempo. It's not a good idea. If you crank yourself with the coffee and use that as the basis of what the tempo of how you think it's going to be, it just doesn't work out quite as well that way, because your staccato rhythm, 'uh uh uh uh uh', has a tendency to irritate people, especially over the phone. But anyway, in general, you want to be able to take your intonation and realize people process language by the phrase so the reasons they put comma's, colon's and periods in language is so that you will stop, and put a space in between.

Now if you add to that fact, that in English, if you change your intonation and flex it to go up, across or down it changes the word you say. (See Figure 2) So that, if you say in English, when you go intonation up, "Ma?" it's a question; then you go intonation flat across, "Ma" it's a statement; and intonation down, "Ma!" it's a command. In Vietnamese, those are three different words, so we have it made. In Vietnamese, in order to make something a com-

INTONATION

SENTENCE QUESTION
SENTENCE STATEMENT
SENTENCE COMMAND

Figure 2

mand, Vietnamese salesman are going to have a lot of trouble compared to us.

Go through a list of all the bad stuff and you want to make sure that you inoculate people against it, not induce it. Here's a great line, "Well I know that you may feel that this is too expensive." "What?" "It's only money. Think about it, it's only made out of paper, it's just your hard work flattened out right into a little thing so that you can open it back up into a world of opportunity. Now if you skip all those opportunities and wait until you're old, you might die and miss them all. It happens. I know people that lived until they were going to retire and when they retired they just ended up leaving their money to ungrateful children. Got teenagers?" That's the first question I ask people, "You got teenagers?" Cause I know where they live now. I go, "Spend it before they do." I go, "Just buy everything you can, before it's too late," because otherwise . . . you know what happens.

My daughter is in college and I went to college then and it wasn't that expensive, now, it's unbelievable what they sock it to you for, boy. Not only that but once you pay for the tuition, every month they come by with some new bullshit thing and want money from you. They don't now who they are dealing with here. Hey, you know, I get this representative to get you on the phone, right, it's cold calling stuff. This lady says, "Are you Elizabeth's father?" And I said, "Yeah." "How much is this going to cost me?" Go for the end. By the way, one of the things I found out studying, that the relationship is, most of the great sales people constantly test for close. Because a lot of times when you are done, if you go too far you can unsell things. It's very very important.

I love this one guy because he was the king of this. His ability to go through and test for close constantly, because you know you can do this with an embedded question, you go, "I don't know whether you're ready or not to put that ring on your finger and have it be there for the rest of your life." And then you can watch them, because people will answer you nonverbally. When you say I don't know whether or not, you're not asking. Sometimes they will even answer verbally, they'll go, "Well, I just don't know." And I go, "I know you feel like you don't deserve it, but isn't it the truth that you worked so very hard in your life."

Now I also was listening not only to your tempo but your tonality. And Canada's better than most places, just think you can be in New Jersey. Or you can be in Texas, cause sometimes in Texas it's kind of hard to get them to understand you, you've got to change that tonality. And I teach it down in Texas and I tell them, "Well you all have got to understand that not everybody in the world is from Texas, when you have people who aren't from Texas," and they always go, "foreigners?" And I go, "Yeah, foreigners, like people from Alabama. You know, people from Chicago," that there are so many varied tonalities, like I even noticed in Canada, there is quite a variation of intonation patterns. You'll like this one, The first time I went to Canada, to work, I was hired to go to Vancouver to do a hypnosis workshop at a hospital. And they let all of the British doctors sit in the front, and the other doctors had to sit behind them. And the nurses had to sit in the back. And I asked, "Why, do the Brits have problems?" Put an end to that, didn't it? I said, "Oh, is it some kind of emotional thing? I mean are they learning disabled, I mean what's the story here, or are they just more stupid than the rest of the people?" You see there is always a way with your tonality to frame any event or any thing.

Now I asked you to write out a list of objections because we want to take the very things that have gotten in your way all along, because this is where the money is. If any of those things stop you, than you need to know how to turn them around before they occur.

The biggest mistake that people make is that they know an objection is coming and they don't get it ahead of time. I get this especially with people who sell high ticket items. I worked for Cesna Jet for awhile, training them. By the way, the commission on a Cesna Jet is great. You only have to sell one and you don't have to work for three years. Now that's cool. It's selling that one jet that's tough. You know, and I like that, out of the sales people they had there. They had one guy sell 75% of the jets. And the rest of them sold one when people forced them to do it. That's what it was like. They were so horrible, it was unbelievable. You know, people don't walk in and go, "Can I have the $5 million jet over there and I'll take two of these." Unless they were an Arab at the time. Some of those guys, they'll buy stuff even if they can't use it. They didn't know what to do. That's the trouble when you take all the money in a country and give it to twelve people. The economy doesn't rock and roll.

It's like, I don't know about you, I'm still sitting around going, "What happened to that So-Damn-Insane guy?" I'm still a little pissed about this whole thing. The guy steals a country. Like we're not going to notice? And he goes, "Oh no, it wasn't a country, it was actually a province of my country." So they go over and they drop the bombs all over them, we're good at that, because the bombs are smart now. Now, we can drop a bomb like in a window. I think that's pretty cool, that changes everything, doesn't it? I just love that Quadafi guy, "This is the line of death, don't cross it." And then you see a guy at the video game set. "This is the bomb that goes down the driveway," and they drop it right in his front window. And you can hear the pilots up there in the planes sixteen miles away telling him which window it is. And he goes, "No, no, no, the window more to the left, more to the left, yeah right up there, okay that's right. A little bit up . . . up . . . there you go." Bpppp right in the window. Now here's a sales technique. Change your behavior or we'll throw a bomb in your window!

People can get away with this sort of nonsense, and you should be able to think that there is a wider range of availability to you, than the kinds of things that you have been doing so far.

Now, I know some of you, on the inside, get this feeling that gets in the way. It's like, I don't know what it is, but when you were young, you were programmed so much, that something happens in your stomach, right? And this is because you have not really learned to have fun, yet.

So I want to use another technique, because remember, to me, it's always learn to increase your skill and back up and increase your personal power. Now, I want to blow out some of this garbage that gets in your way, so that you can recalibrate to find out what you really should be able to do. Because some of you are just too straight, let's face it. The question is: do you want the money or do you want to keep that cramp in your gut? Because you say to yourself, "vavalaflavada," you get those voices in your head that say, "You better not. You're not going to get away with it." Tell them to shut up. We need to be able to put something inside of you that makes it so that when you go and look at where your limitations are, that you have a device, an automatic device inside your mind, begin to flatten it out. Because, let me tell you how that stuff works. It works exactly the same way a phobia works. Isn't that what it is? You get phobic and you don't do things that would work, therefore you make yourself poor. Isn't that neat? And they'll go, "That's because I am mature." No, it's poor, not mature. See, there is some cool stuff you can do, if you can begin to really open up your ears because while you are talking to yourself, you're not listening. I know this from the way some people carry out the exercises when I give them. Some of you aren't even close. There was a guy in one seminar just yesterday who came in and said, "Well, I'm not allowed to talk, when I move this picture over." And I said, "I never said that." And he said, "Oh, well you know," he said, "We talked about it," and I said, "Uh oh. You guys make it too hard." It's all much easier if you keep your eyes and ears open. And people will point stuff out to you in ways that you wouldn't believe.

When you're finished here, you are going to have a laugh. People do stuff and they point things out, literally. They actually do and they show you, especially if you don't come up and ask if I can help you. Come up with a better line than that one. I usually ask them how they are going to pay. You know I walk up and I go, "Do you have a Mastercard?" And they go, "What?" And I go, "Let me see, do you have a Mastercard, Visa, American Express or are you going to pay cash?" And they'll look at me and they will go, "For what?" And I'll go, "For the opportunity of a lifetime." Would you want to miss the opportunity of a lifetime? Well, do you?"

When I started doing this, I used to actually sell them shit they didn't need. I'd just go in my closet and go, "mmmmmmmmmm-mm." Yeah I sold one person my son. He brought him back; he learned the same thing I did. That kid's expensive. Not only that, he eats noisy. I thought I was noisy. And you can't wake him up once he goes to sleep. Something about kids, they grow up over a recording studio, not alarms nothing. Nothing wakes these kids, its unbelievable. They tried everything, like when they were in high school, they'd stack like four and five alarm clocks up. And in the morning I'd hear "Bring, bong, bring, bong," all this noise. And I would be like three flights up. And I'd come down and I'd go in there and these things are going off and they are sleeping away. Can't wake them. And anywhere my son goes, the room turns into a mess. He doesn't have to do anything, he just sits on the couch and the stuff in the room moves.

Now, what I want you to do is I want you to sit back and I want you to close your eyes in just a minute and I want you to pick something that you know you should've done and you couldn't. I want you to locate that knot in your gut that gets in your way. Go back to a time and a place where you thought there was something you should've said, something you should've done. Or just thought of doing something crazy. Because if you can begin to break out of this rut . . . a lot of this is just because you were programmed in school and you were programmed by your parents and all that "you'll be embarrassed" stuff.

Localize *where* the voice in your head *comes from.* Let it keep going and turn the volume up. Make that knot tight. Because you should do it really well for the last time. Enough is enough. And then what I want you to do is, instead of visualizing what did happen from the point you are where you get the knot big and tight, to begin to run the memory backwards. I want you to be able to hear the voice in your head rewind like a tape recorder. I want you to walk backwards, talk backwards and have everything rewind just like a movie moving backwards in a camera. Move way back before the events started. Then I want you to add another voice inside your mind. I want you to have one that goes, "Oooooooo, cool." And I want you to feel something swelling up in the insides of your legs. And I don't care if you are a man or woman, it's purely an attitude adjustment. And I want you to say inside your head as you look at this person, "Your ass is mine."

And I want you to feel something, a pull, because if you rewind things you get to do them in a new way. I want you to hear yourself start to laugh inside your head. You feel tingling spread all over your body. I want you to feel the compulsion to do whatever it is and then let the movie run forward. Feel yourself walking through it, talking through it, listen to yourself. Let your unconscious learn because what you've just been doing is a technique that tells your mind, "Not this, this." First you rewind what you don't want, let it fade away. Then you set your mind in the right direction, and as it moves forward never make the sound "uh uh," always make the sound "Yummm, ahhhh," and let your mind roll forward and begin to run scenarios. Try it one way in your mind, try it another. Keep adjusting it.

Each time I want you to go back to the beginning and run through it. I want you to feel giddier, and more tingling until you begin to see and hear what it is that you can do, that would work for you. Run these things in your mind, over and over and trying different variations, adjusting your tonality, adjusting your tempo. Slow down the rate of your speech. Try speeding it up. Adjust the scenario in your mind, move closer and closer to the target you're after.

Your voice tone, your voice tempo, your physical movements all affect your behavior and attitude. You need one really good outlandish one. Even if it's something you really wouldn't do because it wouldn't work for you. But run a scenario that's just wild. Amuse yourself. Every once in awhile, they turn out not to be so wild. Think of the things that I did that worked. I never thought that people would respond well, but I went ahead and did it anyway to find out. Now, they go, "Thank you, Bob, for selling me a car."

Certainly, you can expand the range of what it is that you are willing to consider. It's always a major surprise, how flexible you can be. If you adjust and put a smile on the face of the people that come around and if you make them feel good, make them feel comfort, and make them laugh, they will always want to come back and they will always want to bring people back with them. They will always want to bring people to try new things and to do it in new ways.

Now I want you to run this scenario and then another one and another one and another one. Let yourself just relax, take a deep breath and let your unconscious maybe show you a few variations that you want to try. Do this until you can make yourself laugh. Because if you make yourself feel good, then the better you feel with each new thing that you try in your mind . . . you're going to teach your unconscious that it's time to try more new things, to do things in new ways and you will have an outrageous attitude, have most "grandes huevos." Because it is throughout the adjustment of beginning to have a bolder and a bolder attitude, that you are going to begin to make more and more money. And using that imagination of yours, to begin to come up with a hundred, a thousand different things you can try. But even in the scenarios inside your mind it is important to listen to your voice tempo. Listen to how resonant your voice sounds, change it so it sounds more and more resonant.

If you do telephone work, I want you to pick up a phone, feel it, hit that receiver and when you speak change your voice so that the tempo is more discrete, put spaces between each and every word. Remember, if you hear them breath you have the opportunity to speak at the rate they are breathing. Remember, you can use all downward, reflections. And this opens up the command module in the mind. Because downwards inflection is the very thing that gets the mind to know that any spoken utterance whatsoever is a command, not a question. You don't want to use a lot of questions. You want to use embedded commands. And I don't know whether or not you know exactly what an embedded command is. But you can stop and say to yourself, "I don't realize just what it could be," but possibly you are learning. You are learning at the unconscious level, and the conscious level, as well, because they need to work together, in a way where it does new things.

What I'd like you to do now is, I'd like you to run a few scenarios in your mind and when you feel you're getting your brain headed in the right direction, and you notice that, when you consider these things in your mind, you don't get a knot, because you don't not need that . . . never. And before you try and stop yourself from preventing the fact that it's not really necessary to do such nonsense, you can remember a time when you did something and you just had to laugh because the only reason you got knots like that, is cause you are nuts in the head. Because you learned to do it and if you can learn to do anything that stupid you can learn to do something new. After all, it's the difference between furniture and human beings.

Now if you don't think you can learn to do something new, then become a couch. And remember I have a black belt in gestalt therapy. Keep it in mind.

Now I want to add the following elements to what you did before. I want you to change your tonality. I want you to slow down. Hear your tempo. When you speak to somebody, if you really want to impact them . . . if I talk really fast and I start talking about my product and making pictures in my head and talking to myself, you lose total contact. Remember, most of the time, you tell people nine times more than you need to. The trick is to remember this rule of thumb. My sales training program goes like this: Induce wanton buying state, then point to product. So if you haven't got the state, you're not ready.

And there's no hurry to get there, but when you ask people questions, I ask them embedded questions and I get my answers non verbally most of the time, which is good enough for me. When they walk in, they walk up and you ask them how ready are they. I don't ask them "Can I help you?" Give me a break, especially if you are calling on the phone.

Somebody talked about how they sell a service, an advertising service and then they have to go and renew it. Sometimes it hasn't worked that well. So they have to take over for somebody else and go in where the other person has sold them and it hasn't worked so their question to me is, "What do you do?" And my response was, "Tell them that's why you're there instead of the other person. Because the company cares about them and wants to get them somebody that will really get them the full impact of the service that's working for so many other people."

Now, one of the most powerful words you can learn by the way, "now." You don't even need context for it. When you stop it's a uniquely individual word and it marks things off. It also sets up the ability for you to begin to connect together things which aren't.

Now, when you begin you want to make sure that you are inducing a very intensely pleasurable state. When you have somebody there and you're talking about something, you're inducing desire. Think about it passionately. I even use all those predicates because I just find that they work very well.

I like to use words like sumptuous. When you show somebody something, whether it's a car or a copy machine, use words like sumptuous or sleek, glistening. I always tell people I go, "Glisten up for a minute." Leave a pause for them to respond. When you see you are getting a good response, stop for a second, let them bathe in it. Especially when you are showing them good things, even if it is a brochure and you hand it to them. Don't tell them they can read it later. Read it to them. It age regresses them. Use that kind of tonality that you would use with a kid just a little bit. People like it. It makes them feel good. You do want to feel good don't you?

Now you have to make your tonality this way. When you are starting to think about things you're going, "Well, um, um, um, uh, uh, ah, oh." I want you to listen on the outside and you want to smooth it out.

This time, I want you to make sure you use all three major representational systems. Overlap from one to another. You say, "Wow," you look down at that diamond ring, "You don't know, yet, what it's going to feel like when it slides onto your finger." The other thing is, when you use words, you squeeze the juice out of them. Every single word has impact. Let it have it. When you have a word like sleek, sound like it. Don't go "It's really sleek, man." You know, you don't say to somebody, "This car has got a really smooth ride." Go, ". . . smoooooth ride."

Now, you may not think you are doing this. But when you come in and you go, "You can have a lot of confi fi fidence in our ser ser service to be one of the b b b best . . ." Well, maybe it's not that exaggerated, but I've got news for you. In a few cases it was just like that. Remember, if you find yourself starting to be nervous, you're not in a good state.

We notice that when we teach this, a lot of you do these exercises during the exercise and then during the breaks, it seems that it's not important or something. These things are in life. Do these things all the time. It's like saying, "Well, I use my NLP in my therapy with my clients, but I didn't know I was supposed to use it on myself." That's one of the problems we don't need to solve. It's like when people say, and I know you know some, "Well, gee, I guess I forgot to use my NLP skills, huh?" Well maybe they should wire in to forget to be ignorant of the fact that they need to use their own brain all the time in ways that are prosperous, healthy, satisfied, motivated, and all the other things they want to be doing. It's like I tell people. They come and say that they want to make more money, or they want to have more happiness, or love, or whatever. That's not what all this is about. When you thrill yourself and live your life excitingly moving in a forward direction you'll find that other people will want to be around, give you opportunities, pleasure, and all the other "things" you want. Living is the experience of processing and NLP is the means for doing it, something which, if we had learned it more explicitly earlier, we wouldn't have this book, or any other, for that matter. NLP isn't a "thing" you use. It's a means for you to learn how to run your own brain. Period. All the time, because if you run your own brain *all the time* so that you get what you want out the life you're living, you wouldn't have to solve so many problems. You'd be able to create more opportunity than you could handle, then, you'd have to give some away because there would so much more. But then you'd have to find people who would want to take those opportunities of a lifetime and then you'd be selling . . . and if you don't do this everyday then you'll have get a different job. If you don't go into those states, fire off those anchors, thrill yourself up, when you first get up in the morning, then you'll have to figure out how to make it through the day, instead of making it the best day of your life each and every day. Wake up in the morning and go, "Life is good. Life is wonderful. And today . . . is the best day for me to be living life to its fullest . . ."

Connect it all together, so that you can be in a good state and talk at the same time. Either that or you'll learn one state. And it's not that productive. So this time take a deep breath go inside, crank yourself up and when you come out, use every word like it's a diamond. Place them perfectly. Make sure you take every word and squeeze everything you can get out of the intonation. When you say, "It's a *wonnnderfuul* opportunity." It's really different than "it's a wonderful opportunity."

"It's a ch ch ch chance of a life time." Don't sound like Porky Pig, he never sold anything. Get in there. Really open your ears. Remember, you don't have to touch your nose and your throat and your chest, just feel yourself do that. Go into state and line it up. Listen, make sure that you're bathing them in tonality. It's going to make it so that they yield desire. Once you do that, start to crank it up.

Remember, you want to know where those pictures are. You want to know, because every moment you want to make sure you put your product in the right place. I saw someone putting it in the place where the person was getting agitated. I don't know, it was either that or they had bad breath or something. But in either case, they were standing far too close. Get yourself a little distance, stand to the side, until you know where things are and grab a hold of them. Draw the picture where you want it to be. Remember, if you draw the picture and you put in the representational system visually, overlap to the auditory and get into those kinesthetics because that's where the real buying decisions are made. If people don't feel right they *may* do it but they will not be happy and most of the time they will bring it back and you will spend a lot of time screwing around with them. Make sure that when you close a sale in such a way that when they do come back, they feel obligated to bring you someone with them.

The sale isn't over until the customer comes back and brings someone with them.

You know, I've had tons of people who came back and said, "Hey, you got any of those Cadillac's left?" This is in the middle of the oil crisis, when people couldn't give them away. I'd look in the paper, there would be fifty of them and they would still be there weeks later. And the reason is because they didn't know how to induce the state where somebody put their priorities in the right order. The right order is that safety is more important than saving a few bucks. I mean, how many of you guys would drive around in a car that you could get killed in to save ten dollars a week? Is that it? How many of you like spending money, because you know what a water pump for one of those little small things cost in the middle of the oil crisis? A water pump was $300 bucks! Oh, you mean parts are hard to come by? And by the way, have you ever tried to work on a car where the engine is bigger than the hood? Even to take a spark plug out, you had to be a contortionist. You had to be able to make your hands, your wrists and your elbows bend in all directions. Plus you had to go out and buy new tools because it was metric. I saved those people a lot of money. Most of them probably still have the car. But they brought people back, I even got calls after I moved.

I moved to San Francisco where I always lived. And I moved to San Francisco because I discovered that I was not a country person, by the way. Many people are country people but I went into the country and simply began to organize it into the city. I got generators and stuff. There was a big snow storm on the mountain that I lived on. Huge snow storm, snow fell more than it had fallen in twenty years. A million trees fell down, and knocked out all the power . . . for three weeks. And I still had television, a heated swimming pool. And there was just one big building on the top of the mountain that glowed, I had people march out in the snow and ask if they could come in and get warm, and they'd come in and my stereo was blaring away. I had a big gas stove. I had people sleeping in my living room. And people would ask, "Where are you getting the electricity?" And I said, "From the sun. Isn't that where everybody gets it from?" And they said, "No, we get ours from Pacific Gas and Electric company." And I said, "They charge for theirs." And that so aggravates me. I like it where you get a check from them every month. I don't know if they have it in other parts of the world but in the US, if you can generate more electricity than you use, the meter runs backwards and they have to pay you. You put a wind mill on top of your house. And it generates more electricity than you use. PG& E has to send you a check every month. And they had to tell me that just one time. That was all it took, hey that's the best sales of all. They have to buy it whether they want it or not. That's like the book of the month club. Same deal, right? And the thing is every month they sent me a check and I had more electricity than any-body, I had wind power, sun power, I even had a fossil fuel plant of my own. I'd burn up anything that I could find. Anything I burned up, I made it so that it made the windmill go around. It's like all these things, I had on top of the mountain and I had an indoor tennis court. Because I don't like the sun.

You know there's a hole in the sky. Did you know that? Isn't that something? There is a hole in the sky. And I've had people, "Oh no, let's go lay out on the beach." That's why the aliens don't land because they are convinced that we are not the intelligent life form on this planet. We work for our pets, not only that but they eat us. They do, you go out on the beach in Hawaii and there they are on the beach cooking. They put oil on them and everything. What would you think if your were coming down from the sky? The easiest way to enter the earth's atmosphere is over Australia because of the way the earth spins. So if you come down across Australia, and then you come down and you go across Hawaii on your way to California, you go across the Hawaiian Islands, they are cooking people on every beach there. Then when you get to California they are boiling them in their back yard. It's got to look that way, that's why the aliens, they're not talking to us, unless they are hungry. It's got to be that way. Your point of view will always be your point of view.

Now, I'd like you to stop for a minute, and I want you to go back and think about that reference client. I want you to go inside, and find out if they are beginning to look more like a meal. I like to cover mine with chocolate. I see chocolate dripping off of them. It doesn't matter what angle their at. Like even people sit-ting in a seminar where they always have to sit in the same seat. I always loved that, because some people can only get knowledge in if they are only sitting in one chair. Otherwise the knowledge just won't go in. You think I'm kidding don't you? I'm not actually. If you think about submodalities and where those little windows are, that's why because people can't sit in a particular chair, they have to go one back and one over. It's the angle of opportunity.

Now, if you stop and you think about that client now, I want you to think about doing something outrageous. We want you now to combine all of the things that we've been putting together into a package and begin to run scenarios in your mind. You see we want to turn this around, so that when the client looks at you, they say the magic phrase.

You see you have to have the look inside your eyes. Keep in mind for a minute, have you ever been up close to an eagle. Do you know that look that eagles, have in their eye? It's a look that just unnerves you, where they don't blink. They look deep into your soul. And you need to have a little bit of the look of the eye of the eagle inside of you. You need to be able to make sure that you have that look that won't miss anything because it's inside of yourself. You begin to formulate a feeling based on it. To know what it's like to look out and to make it so that when you look at things, it almost burns the soul of the person that you are looking at.

See, if you step inside an eagle and you begin to look down at your client, it doesn't mean that you have to give up the feeling of the big cat. Because what I want to form for you is a little bit of what we call a "will of steel." If you take for yourself, that just at this moment, begin to feel something very solid sliding down inside of you. Something that will build utter and complete determination. Because one of the things you need to have is almost like a homing device, because if you let your eyes . . . feel right from behind them . . . and then something . . . that piercing comes from the back of your eyes and the front of your eye begin to look out and look down at that client. From the inside of your body I want you to stretch out and feel your claws and then slowly let something slide down the top of your head. All the way down to your feet. Something solid, something determined, and something that once its inside you, never gives up.

I found out people give far too easily. But if you feel that coming down just let it slide down and go shhhhhpt, and feel it lock in. Something that does not give up, something that can bend a little bit, but always springs back. And something surrounded with your sense of humor. Because I want you to keep in mind that, every client that you have trouble with is your university. When I talked earlier about how stupid I think it is that they don't give degrees in salesmanship, they don't give degrees in Persuasion Engineering™ . . . but they give degrees in poetry, they give degrees in every bizarre thing you can imagine. It's unbelievable to me, the things that they think are important, the things they think are academic to substance. Now, I guess that's why they call it an academic education. Because its irrelevance is not always aimed at accomplishing the things in life that I think are vital. But if you begin to feel something swirl around and around that wheel of steel and begin to build up inside of you, I want you to feel it so that it spreads right down to your finger tips. It locks in behind your jaw, and the voice in the back of your head can reverberate and say, "Their ass is mine." Because that's the point at which they will become the university of life.

When I see other people where I would know their techniques they would become my university. They became the person who would increase the range of my flexibility. That's where you get to go, "Ahhhhh. This is a rare and unprecedented opportunity to do something new." Because if you know that the things that you have done thus far don't work, you need to be able to vary your behavior.

Now, I'd like to go back to the example of when I was talking about the head hunter. We played the tape from this guy, who spoke slower than was humanly possible. Now, the guy that was trying to get this guy to change his position, told me he couldn't even get an appointment with this guy. So what he did was he played the tape, and I walked up and I handed him a towel. And I said, "You must match this guy's tonality, and tempo. You can't speak faster than he has." The guy looked at me with fear in his eyes and he said, "I don't think I can talk that slow." And I said, "Fake it." I pressed the redial button on the phone and began to dial, it rang, the guy picked it up and said, " Hello" and the guy that I was doing the training with went, "Helllooo, Bob," and began to strain In fact, I had to pass towels out to everyone in the room because they were laughing so hard, tears were coming out of their eyes. But within a matter of minutes, suddenly, this guy had an appointment. This guy could only process information at the rate that he could speak it. Now, you've started doing things that had to do with ambiguities, you've learned that "I shot an elephant in my pajamas," has more than one meaning. That as you begin to realize that you can deliver simultaneous messages, that when you can say to people things in a variety of ways and the impact that it could actually have double meanings . . . And a little fairy tale called the <u>Adventures of Anybody</u>, is a fairy tale in which there is a whole chapter that runs where it could be two stories. And it is the output of learning to master language. He talks about how Anybody walked in a room and fell into what he did not know. That's a pretty broad ambiguity. He then fell all to pieces. He looked. He was ahead of himself. And suddenly there he was, beside himself with fright. You know your ability to master language and use it, to use what is called the Milton Model . . . every single language distinction, begins to add to you a whole new domain. We talked about embedded questions and I don't know if you realize how important they can be. I don't know if you understood that that was an embedded question. Just like this is. Embedded questions are very powerful, because what they do is they elicit responses without verbal answers. Because one of the things you always want to do is to build up response potential. It's almost like building a dam in the Cyber River inside of a human being, so that it builds up, so that when you open the gate, it flows out with force. Now, I don't know whether or not you realize just how important this can be. But I know that you're beginning to understand. Really understand it. Because when you understand, you will realize that it's not just that you can build it up with embedded questions, isn't it? It's that you can use tag questions, can't you? to do the same thing.

Now Gregory Bateson, who actually asked me to write <u>Patterns</u> and went around with Milton, when I read it to him, actually I gave him the manuscript and he read the book, he told me, "Richard, this is shoddy epistemology." And I said, "What do you mean, Gregory?" And he said, "You can't use a pattern to teach a pattern." And I said, "You can't, can't you?" And he said, "If you do, it violates logical levels." And I said, "That's all right, I don't give a shit." What I care about is that the human ear begins to develop recognition, because performance and production of human beings aren't the same things. Human beings first learn to hear. Then they learn to say. Human beings can hear when they are children, and understand much more than they can produce in language. Now that mechanism is alive and well inside of each of you, is it not? As you begin to change what it is that you are capable of hearing, and let that wheel of steel begin to grow and hear it come all the way and lock in outside yourself. You begin to find that you can become more and more and more aware of what there is to hear. You see most people think words just shoot across the room and bound into someone's ear. It's not just that, you also have the ability to bathe someone in tonality simultaneously. You want the tonality that you use to be capable of creating both the phenomenon where they are attracted to it and the phenomenon where they are repulsed away from it. Where people say, "Well, I have to go and look at every single kind of car." You always want to go, "eeeewww," Because that sound which builds aversion, try saying it and go, "eeeewww." I also find that that this (yachk) is very useful as well. I always go, "You know it's not that important that you look at every car, isn't it? It's just not that important." And as you begin to use language to build responses with people, and they go, "Well, I was going to look at the Volvo, the Jaguar and the Mercedes." And I go, "Oh, the Jaguar. That's not very a good car, you know what I mean?" You'll begin to build aversions at what it is that constitutes your competition.

I always know that when I owned a restaurant, people would come in and think it was the one across the street. And I'd go, "eeewww, but they have a salad bar in that place." People go, "Yeah," and I go, "Eeeeewww, do you know what's in salad bars? People come by and blow germs in it, touch it with their hands, and then you put that stuff in your mouth? Oh yuk! It's not exactly the best thing." You'd be surprised you can build a phobia in an instant. There's not only their germs but there're cooties as well. And you have to be careful of cooties at all times.

You see, when I took people out and I showed them a used car and I walked by and I went, "This is Ralph, this is Peter," Ralph didn't actually run. Ralph was a Volvo. And I kept the Volvo around because when I'd tell people, I'd say, "I'd like to show you, if you are going to go buy a Volvo where you are going to be." And I take them out into the back and I'd actually concocted something in my laboratory, it smelled so bad, you couldn't believe it. It was something really foul. It's not like a new car spray smell. Quite the opposite. Such, that when they opened the door, that smell would shoot through their body and build an aversion. And I would always simultaneously say, the word "Volvo." I'm sure the Volvo people are going to love me, when this comes out, don't you think? But it's not the new Volvo's, it's just the old ones. Before Volvo was sold to another company they became the lemon kings of cars.

Now, when I did this to build aversion, I did it because I knew that when I showed people these things, that I would be able to install in them a response that would aim them to the right direction, away from my competition and towards me. It's important that you build a propulsion machine. Propulsion machines are those things that push and pull at the same time. Now I want to build a propulsion machine inside of you and the propulsion machine I want to make . . . something that you know how to install at all times . . . and that's one that moves to success. See if right now, inside your mind, you begin to feel it start to rain money, because you hear a funny noise, you begin to look around in your mind and you notice $100 bills are raining out of the sky. And you look over and you realize that you can pick up as many of those as you want when you finish with that client over there. So in your mind look at them and start to move towards them and see the fear in their face. See the money, falling faster, harder, building up around you actually having to trudge through it. Pick up one of the bills and smell that new money smell. It's so distinctive, there's nothing like the smell of freshly printed money. And begin to stick in your pocket. Because the closer that you get to that client. The more of this you are going to get. Because if you walk over and walk behind that client, put your hand on their shoulder and say to yourself, "Ha ha ha ha, their ass is mine." You will begin to adjust your attitude in a direction that moves towards success.

Now, if you look back at how you were before, look back across the ravine and see yourself actually being afraid of this client and laugh and realize how easy it is to change, and say to yourself, maybe I'll go back and be the person that I was yester-day. You know you can, you can leave this here, and forget every-thing that you knew. And for each step you start to take back-wards, I want you to feel a hot poke in the ass. Because that would be just what it would be like to begin to step backwards, into the inflexibility you had towards just this client.

See they constitute an opportunity, because once you conquer them, you conquer a whole world of new clients. You increase your close ratio, you end up having new flex ability. Because usu-ally, there's not just one that's like them. There's a whole bunch that are just like them. Those are the ones that you have trouble dealing with. They may not be the ones that somebody else does, but all the ones that you are successful with, they are a piece of cake. It's all the ones that you haven't been able to connect with, yet, because you haven't learned to vary your tonality, your tempo, your behavior, even just the polarity responders, the ones that no matter what you say, say "Yes" they say "no," say "no," they say "yes," but, some of those are tough for people. Not for me, I go, "You can't buy this car." And they go, "Yes, but I want it." You see, you can turn anything around.

CHAPTER SIX

HOLOGRAPHIC DYNAMICS

You see, after you've got their attention and establish rapport and gather information, you have to be able to put their presentation together in your mind. Now I like to do this as we go because it's so easy and I do like to take the easiest way to do things, as long as it works well.

See, when you build your presentation of propulsion, including those things they want, need, like to have, the tonality that goes with these, the direction to go buy and the roadmap to success, you collect the information first, by asking questions that get the information, then being sure that you have a way of encoding it to remember it yourself. I do this by building a map, seeing what they're seeing and saying what they're saying, and doing what they're doing, and testing these enough to know that I've got it. And the better you get, the more you get and the easier it is so start now. Remember, it often doesn't take very much to move it along but you have to do it.

It's like let's take the real estate business, for example. I just had a friend of mine today call me and I asked how well he's doing and he said, "I'm great!", even though the market is slow. There are still people buying, they're just being more thoughtful before making their decisions. So he tells me how easy it is for him and I asked him, of course, how he's doing it. He says, "I give them what they want in a way that lights them up vivaciously."

So, here we are in a selling situation where we want to demonstrate just one simple example about how to engineer influence purposefully and quickly.

The salesperson, Charlie (all names have been changed to protect the engineers and engineered), has his desk right in front of the the office by a window, where he can see out front when people drive up in their cars. All this information for free, you don't even have to ask for it, just to get started.

This couple drives up, gets out of their car, and looks around. The woman points to one of the homes across the street and he looks. They say something to each other (this is where lip reading comes in handy). They walk across the street and look at the house from different angles, she's nodding up and down and he's moving his head side to side across his shoulders slightly. They turn, begin to cross the street and they both stop and look at the house next door. Then they go over there. Charlie, by the way, goes into the next room where he can more easily observe them. They walk around the house and when they come back to where they started they're both smiling, almost laughing, there's Charlie starting to go outside, when they come in.

Charlie greets them with, "You really like the one next door, huh?"

Charlie has their attention and wants to keep them in what he considers to be an already existing good state.

He: "Yeah, we've kinda been looking around, you know, and we saw your company here so we thought we'd stop and look here."

Charlie starts matching the pace of the customer's breathing and rhythm. He also notes that his question isn't answered directly but they're both smiling again like when they were next door.

C: "Well, I'm wondering, exactly what will do it for you today."

Uses an embedded question and lays out a time frame.

He: "We really have to find a new home soon. Our lease is up and we don't want to get stuck extending it. We're ready for this and want to make the best of our investment."

Note the "have to" operator and "don't want" which Charlie can use to build the propulsion later. Also note the "want" to and what follows it, i.e. investment. There's also a signal to timing: "ready."

C: "So how can I make the best of your investment work for you? What does your new home here have to have?"

Charlie paces and then uses the "have to" operator to to elicit more information connected to this.

He: "Well, as we look down the road, we want to be sure we have something with resale value. We also may plan on just staying here when we raise our own family so . . . we *need* at least three bedrooms, maybe four, we *need* two full baths, we *want* a large living room, an eat-in kitchen and a basement. We would also *like* to have a fireplace and a patio would also be nice."

Notice the reference here to timeline and direction and the modal operator of possibility "may". Then he starts his modal operators linked to the specific criteria content: need, then want, then like-to-have. Charlie carefully maps these out according to how the customer maps them out with his analog movements linked to each of these. (See Figure 3)

She: "And we also *need* a laundry room and *need* lots of closet space. We *don't want* to be cramped in anymore."

Note here the addition to the "need" modal operator linked to more specified criteria content. Charlie also notes this customer's analog information that is linked. He also notes that the guy nods his head here in agreement with her. Also the "don't want" will

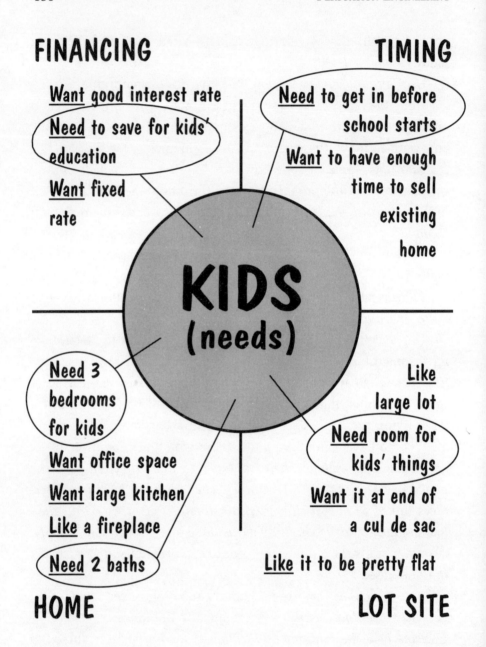

Figure 3

become important for building the propulsion later.

C: "Let me see if I got this right. You *need* three bedrooms, maybe four and you *need* two full baths. You also *need* a laundry room and lots of closet space. You *want* a large living room, an eat-in kitchen and a basement. And you'd *like* to have a fireplace and a patio."

Now Charlie gives back the modal operators linked to the specified criteria, including the analogs exactly as they were presented to him (mirrored to the same exact place for them) and even nods his head back to the guy when presenting her information back to her.

Both: "Yup"

(Yes Response!)

C: "And as you look down the road, this will have a good resale value and been a good investment, even if you plan to stay here and raise your family?"

Charlie starts to link these into the timeline as described by them.

Both: "Yup."

(Another Yes Response!)

She: "Ohhhh, and we really love those cathedral ceilings, if you have them."

Charlie notes the short breathing in and the tonality that goes with the smile and obvious skin color deepening as she adds this criteria. She also points both her arms up toward the ceiling in connection with this.

C: "Ohhhh, great, you'll love the ones we have here."

And he matches it back exactly, except for raising his arms toward the ceiling (And I'm wondering why not)

Both: "Can we take a look at the house now?"

Charlie notes their speech change to a more rapid rate with increased volume in their voice.

C: "Ohhhh, of course, you're going to love this one, let's go by the house right now . . ."

Charlie uses the same match as the previous one and this time as he says "let's go by (great phonological ambiguity, buy the way) the house right now, he matches back her analogs to the cathedral ceiling.

Now, as these two people light up, by the way, this is great. I've seen this guy in action before, but this gets better.

He's not satisfied with this alone because he's had many customers who have changed their minds once they get back to their friends and families, or whatever, so he continues to elicit more information from them. You see, we want to begin to connect as much as we can to whatever feeling it is that will override anything else. This may also be very useful later, if we need it to override any slight objections that Charlie may not have inoculated against (this is a big ticket purchase).

So Charlie begins to ask questions around the already presented information so he can gather even more. Now, this information is valuable and Charlie knows that each and everytime he asks for more and valuable information, he's going to have to keep track of how much he gives back, in terms of information. The reciprocating effect of information exchange is important. I learned this by watching and listening in on a few interactions where the salespeople kept asking for information and didn't offer anything back. It was like an interrogation or something. It's like, "So what kind of house do you want? How many rooms? How much do you want to spend? Do you want a corner lot? Do you have kids? Where do you work?" and other things like this. I mean, after all, the customer is doing more work then they have to. Some people even go for very private information before they've earned the right to it. Like that insurance guy earlier. He asks me for my address, and remember, he's not going to send me anything, right? So why does he need my address. I give him my standard mailing address, a post office box, and this guy goes, well, what's your street address? This is like the second or third question the guy asks me. And I say, "Well, I gave you the best address to mail me information and he goes, "What, do you live in a p.o. box?" and I say, "Yeah, and it's pretty roomy in here, too. We're even thinking about adding an indoor pool." Of course, I'm the one with the attitude, right?

So, Charlie starts asking about the "needs" first, right? Because he knows that most probably, the "needs" *must* be filled. These generally aren't negotiable, although we have seen that change from time to time, depending on their orientation and the point of time. So he says, "So you *need* at least three bedrooms." She says, "Well, four would be better because, if we stay, we'll probably stay for a while. And Greg and I need an extra room anyway for our office." Charlie says, "Office?" (a great way to elicit more information, by the way. Take the last word or phrase of their sentence back as a question.)

She says, "Well yes, we've been operating our own small business on the side, you know, to make some extra money to give us a little flexibility in our investment for our future." Charlie goes, "Gee, that must work out well for you." They respond, "Yeah. It's pretty good. We don't want to keep doing the same old thing like everybody else and we like our freedom, so we thought we'd take a chance on this thing and so far it's worked out well for us. It could even turn into a full time thing for both of us. That would give us a lot of flexibility with our time and everything. We could do more of what we want when we want."

Now inside this conversation is lots of information for Charlie to map and use. (There's a diagram that attempts to illustrate this and we acknowledge that it is a single dimension, single modality illustration and rough at best, but we want to illustrate a way to use this, as an example on paper. The best way, of course, is to map it in your own brain, as you go along). (See Figure 4)

In short, Charlie asks questions in some general areas that are obviously home buying oriented. He can choose from about nine different general areas, and usually is guided first by the customer's desire to go over those areas. Some of these areas may be financial, timing, the home style, interior layout, the community, the site itself, builder history, etc.

So, in your particular business, it would be most useful for you to come up with some areas like these for your business. What sorts of general information do your customers ask for? If you don't have this right now, start keeping track of the questions you are asked. Remember, everytime your customer asks a question, it's the opportunity for you to build your presentation up front later with the next customers, and begin to inoculate against objections. Not that every question is an objection, we're not saying that. We're saying that each and everytime your customer has a question, it's because they may not have an answer *from your company*, and they may already have someone else's answer and are making a comparison. But let's simplify this. Questions are good because they are an opportunity. If you get the same kinds of questions again and again, it's an opportunity.

So, Charlie has these different general areas he can sort through with the customer. We only ask a few types of questions because we want some specific information. We want to know where the majority of the information leads to, especially when it comes to big ticket items. We get very lucky sometimes and it's easy. Then, again, there are times when the customer, likes to have more information than we think they need, but they feel they need it, so we like to be in a position to target it in to where it's useful to both them and us. You know, some people just like to collect information without really using it. If you're going to have

Figure 4

it, use it, or you're wasting their time and yours.

We want to know where the different contexts come together, or tie together so that later on, we can use that to light up all their candles at once.

Here, think about it like this. How many doors do you want to have to open to find out where the prize is? And how many of those doors can lead to the right pathway for reaching the ultimate destination? It's like how easily can you narrow down the window of opportunity so that there is less "slop" and more precision in your engineering influence? There are lots of different ways of narrowing the windows of opportunity. What's important is that you can use just language to narrow this window. It's also interesting to note that the narrower the windows are that the client already has, the more you'll have to work to find the existing window of opportunity. Pretty simple, though, when you watch and listen.

Let's say we want to use the example of where somebody comes in and they begin to present their own representation of what they want, or expect to get from the sale. Based on what they present, notice their physiology, how they stand, sit, head tilts, etc. especially when they're using generalizations, nominalizations, and modal operators. There are, of course, other Meta Model categories, and these are real easy to track. I mean, how they stack these generalizations, and which Meta Programs they're using in the sentence structures can give more information than most people need, or know what to do with, for that matter.

The modal operators, provide a way of prioritizing, or ordering the sequence of things, and if you want to notice how they place along the timeline of the person, you start to notice how many doors the information has to get through to reach them. It's always amazed me that people present what's going on in their brain through their language and how many people have missed it through the years. Ever heard someone say, "Am I getting through to you?" The question I would ask is, "Getting through what?" Well, maybe it's just that we need to know where the windows of opportunity are open or how to open those windows of opportunity.

So, Charlie asks questions about different contexts in his particular business, like the community, the timing, the finances, and each time he goes into that area (of their brain and map) he asks, or uses conversational postulates, or embedded questions as he starts to sort for the opening where heaven waits. He may ask things like, "So you *need* three bedrooms?" And they'll respond, "Well, yeah, we have two kids and they each need their own bedroom. Of, course, four bedrooms would be better, you know." "Oh, of course." Then he'll ask, "And you want a good community, of course." "Well, what we're really interested in is whether or not there are things for the kids to do. You know, where are the playgrounds, what kinds of sports are there, and those things?"

Charlie takes each of the areas he figures are going to be of interest or objection, and begins eliciting the information he needs to build his presentation.

❦ CHAPTER SEVEN:
OBJECTIONS

We want to spend some time working on turn arounds. These turn arounds are where you view limitations. It's the very doorway to success. So I want you to pull out that list of objections. And we are going to do some serious ass kicking here. It's always amazed me. Here was a Mercedes lot and these guys never left it. In all the time they were there, they had no courage. They never got in the car. The only time they would leave is if somebody was nice enough to come in and go for a test drive. And then they'd take a test drive and all they would do is drive around the block. Not me, I'd like to put the top down, and drive up the beach, take a nice long leisurely drive. I'd let them drive and I'd sit in the back seat and go, "You want this, you want this." And they'd go, "I know." And I'd go, "You want this so much."

I know that, think about it, inside of you, each one of you thought of the thing that you absolutely saw and you absolutely had to have it. There wasn't just a picture, there was a voice, too, wasn't there? You remember? Now, where was the voice? Wasn't it most of the time behind you? It seems to be very, very universal. So I like to get behind them and talk. I spend a moment or two, especially if I can learn their intonation pattern. And sometimes it doesn't matter, because a lot of times it's not even their voice. It's somebody telling them whether they can have something. Very often it's a parents voice or a grandparent's voice. It doesn't matter, cause in the future it's going to be my voice. I make sure of that. Now, I flat out ask them, I'll say, "Well when you bought something and you knew it was perfect and you were right, when you made your best decision, where's the voice come from? Is it behind you, in front of you? to the right? to the left?" And they'll stop and go, "I never thought about that." And they'll go, "Well it's kind of back here," which it usually is.

And it has to do within our cultures. We spend so much time on the phone. People go literally into telephone postures. Just like they call up, "Hello, self, are you in there? I want to buy this car, would that be all right? No, you can't buy the car. You must do this, you must do that. Well yeah, but I really like the car." Now, the next time you call yourself, tell yourself to shut up. And have your own way.

But I like to get behind them, because you see there is very little that I can do from the passenger seat, compared to what you can do if you actually sit in the back seat right behind them. Now, I do this with everything. I walk around behind people, because when you sit them in a chair, I don't care if it's insurance, I've sold just about everything there is. Sometimes, I've sold stuff at places I don't even work. You know, I tried it. I had a guy leave his insurance book one night, so I went up and down the street the next day selling insurance, I found out that you can be arrested for that. I said, "Well I didn't take any money." And they said, "Yes, but you misrepresented yourself." I said, "No, I knocked on the door and I said, "I'm not an insurance salesman, but I want to show you something," and I took out the book. Actually I wrote the names down and gave it down to the insurance guy and he went back and still hooked up three of the sales. They already signed on the bottom line. And he went back and he still talked them out of it. That shows me something: Stop when your ahead.

Constantly you want to be able to take your presentation and put in it and ask questions, embedded questions which say things like, "Well I don't know if you are ready to just take this home with you." People nod yes, you get to shut up. Let them buy it if they want to. Don't talk them out of it. Don't be mean, because a lot of times, people were ready to buy something and I guarantee you that you talked them out of it. Because you couldn't stop. "Oh, but I'm only this far in the sales process." *No, anytime you can close, you're done.*

You may want to install a few post hypnotic suggestions. I do. I like to install the suggestion that they will come and they will bring me twenty new people. Actually, once they sign the contract, I pick it up and start to tear it, and I go, "You don't deserve this," and they will grab it out of my hand and they'll say, "Well wait a minute. What's wrong?" And I go, "I don't know, Barbara is not for you." I said, "Look, it's like this, I've managed to sell you something that you really want, what are you going to do for me?" And they go, "Well you work here." And I go, "Sometimes. That's not the point. Don't you know people who deserve to have as good of an opportunity as you do? Don't you care about the human race?" Ruthless line, isn't it? But you have to master ruthlessness. Sometimes you just have to be cruel to be kind. And the more you try to think that's true the more you will. Because it is in it's own way, you see, if you believe in the way that you do things. And I believe that people making the right decision and, having that decision stick inside of them, is the most important things a human being can learn about: your ability to engineer one decision so that they make a good one is going to lead to a lifetime of their engineering good decisions about lots of things. Because when they understand that these are good decisions and these are bad decisions, then they are going to start looking to find out whether the decisions they are making in their life are good ones or are bad ones. What I want you to learn is to start making even better decisions because when you decide to treat somebody you're working with one way, versus another, in essence what you are doing is making a decision which cuts your income to what it is now.

Your income should be twice, four times what it is now. But you make decisions that make you behave in certain ways. That make you sound certain ways. You walk up and you pitch too fast. One of the worst things that most people do is pitch way too fast. Make them feel real good and then bathe your product in it. Bathe your service in it. They need to know that every time you come near them . . . not that they're going to feel like they have their hands down their pants . . . but they feel like they are stepping into a warm bath and it's where they want to be. You want them calling you constantly, finding out if they could spend more money, don't you? How many of you would say, "No, I'm sorry, I won't sell you another one." That's what you are doing if when you're done, they feel like they have been raped.

You see, you can force people into things, but you can't make them get addicted to it. Now, the addiction pattern is something if you want to make yourself the commodity. You want to make it so that it is so much more fun to talk to you on the phone, that they'll call up and buy another one. Now, do you want to talk through your nose anymore? Or do you want to begin to speak from down here (diaphragm)? You want to begin to say hello in a way that makes them go, "Yes!!" That same feeling inside of them, in fact, you want to make it so they internally say yes so many times, don't you, don't you, don't you?! So that inside that embedded question, they go, "Yes, Yes I do." Do you want to feel good? "Yes." The more yeses you can get inside of them the better they are going to feel at every moment. Now, if you have lots of yeses you have the command module open. Then you begin to put in suggestions as any elegant hypnotist would do. And that's not the bozo guy walking across hot fire up there. Tony at least changes your fears in you into something. Change your fears into courage, but you know the other guy, there's another guy now, that just does the fire walk, he doesn't bother with changing your fear into courage. The question is, how many fire walks have you been on? And I don't remember the guy's name, but he came up to me at a thing I did in Denver. He walked up to me and looked me in the eye and said, "I've done forty-five fire walks." And I said, "What's the matter, haven't you gotten it right yet? Because his problem was that he turned his fear into stupidity. The point is to overcome it, not just keep doing it for no reason. Now we have a hypnotist, that has someone walking across broken glass, there's a great decision. Let's all throw bottles down and tap dance on it.

I'm looking for people that when they do something, they have a feeling that stays with them for the rest of their life. When I take somebody out, the best point in the sale of all to me is when they've signed on the dotted line. Because I take them out and I show it to them. And I go, "It's yours forever, no one can take this away from you." And every single time you look at this, you're going to feel good. You're going to know that you made the right decision. You're going to think of this, because you like me, want the best for yourself. You, like me, want the best for yourself and others. So when you think of somebody who has needs, what's going to come to mind? Richard is, except I want it to be you. I don't want you to go out there, get them almost up to the close of sale and then have them call me on the phone.

I have a thing that I do called the wealth concert, because I really think that people need to be trained to appreciate wealth. And most people, when they get it, it either makes them paranoid, or they become stupid. I mean, they just don't know how to deal with it, that they don't know how to bathe themselves in success, or once they start to become successful, they cease working. They don't realize that's the time to pour it on. You can actually get ahead. On your shoulders too.

Now the thing about the wealth concert, that I like to do is, I like to get people into the idea that what they are about to do is going to change everything forever. It's the best decision you could make. A decision to be successful. Let's see, when you make a decision, when you look at your decision thing, it in essence works the same way a post hypnotic suggestion works. How many of you decide what to get at the store, write it down, don't bring the list and get everything? I'm like that, I always forget the list, but never anything on it. Some people just have to write things down to remember them. Look around, see the people with the note pads, they are not going to read these notes. It's just how they write in their head. Some of you just write it down directly.

I've started doing it now, because I can't find a pen most of the time. My dog takes them. She's got a whole collection under the bed. I can't get under the bed, it's too small. So she has all my things down there. She goes and holds them just out of reach. She goes, "You, ha ha ha ha, you work for me." I also have bought one of those beds that doesn't have wheels and is made out of very heavy wood. I bought a mattress that's so heavy I can barely flip it over. So to lift the bed up, I can lift it but I can't crawl under it at the same time. But next time I get a bed, I want hydraulics so I can press a button and it goes, nnnnnnnt. How many of you would like to press a button and have your bed go up towards the ceiling so that nobody could bother you? On the other hand, what some of you need is a bed that's high like that and then tilts out in the morning, when your alarm clock goes off.

And everybody always asks me, "How do you overcome objections?" And my answer is, "You don't." Not if you are good at this.

If you know what the objections are going to be, you inoculate them so they never occur.

I make that part of the presentation and people say, "Well they always tell me it's too expensive," and so I'm bound in my presentation to talk about how "idiots think that the price of this, the people who are totally idiotic think that this is too expensive . . . but what they don't realize" and then you can bring up things.

For example, you know, how many cars do you want to buy in the next ten years? How many vacuum cleaners do you want to own? How many times do you want to buy a stereo? Or do you want to buy something and be partially dissatisfied with it because every time you use it, it breaks on you? Or do you want to do it once and do it right? After all, you know, you get what you paid for in the sense, not that you pay less money because in the long run you can pay more money.

One of the things I've always thought is that I hate buying junk. Because I end up buying it again. How many of you have bought many of the same product because you never bought a good one? Think about it. If you sell good products, you'll get good results. If you are one of those people that sell junk, you'll have to come up with another line. You'll have to come up with hey, you know, its like making payments but getting a new one every year. Think about it, you can have a new car every three years or one car for ten years. all right, at the end of the ten years, the good car will be worth something. The other ones, you'll have had the satisfaction of knowing that there aren't cooties in your car.

Cooties are a powerful part of sales. Do you have cooties in your country? Do you know what those are? Ahhhhh, mmmm-mmm, see this all started in elementary school. Don't you remember that people of the opposite sex had cooties? Well, now psychics have taught me that there are cooties, alright. And what cooties are is that when you buy a used car it's got somebody else's vibes on it. So the trick is not to not have vibes on it, it's to make sure that when you sell them a used car, that it has good vibes on it.

After all, if a creep drove the car, the good smell won't last forever, but to sort through and pick out which of the cars your going to sell then do what I do. What you do is you show them two you know they won't want, the absolutely worst choices for them so they are ready and frustrated and then say well there is one other one, but I don't think you'll like it. And then put them in something which is perfect and let them force you to sell it to them. And fight them every inch of the way. They go "Oh no, no I like this, this is perfect." "You don't have to say that just to make me feel better." People, say, "Well, I would never do that." Like they really would you know. And go, "Hey, I'm not that desperate, you know. I could take you to another car lot. You know, you could put up with their lying ways." I actually used to take my clients, sometimes to other car lots, because if we didn't have anything that I thought was right for them, I would go over and negotiate for them with the other salesmen. They hated that. Because I could get the price way down. In fact I could get them down on their knees if I wanted to. They go, that's not fair, and I go that's right, but all's fair in sales. Is it not now.

Again, it's important that you build a propulsion machine. Propulsion machines are those things that push and pull at the same time. (See Figure 5)

Now I want you to build a propulsion machine inside of you and, I want you to make something that you know how to install at all times. And that's one that moves to success. Right now,

Figure 5

inside your mind, begin to feel it start to rain money . . . because you hear a funny noise, you begin to look around in your mind and you notice $100 bills are raining out of the sky. And you look over and you realize that you can pick up as many of those as you want when you finish with that client over there. So in your mind look at them and start to move towards them and see the fear in their face. See the money, falling faster, harder, building up around you actually having to trudge through it. Pick up one of the bills and smell that new money smell. It's so distinctive, there's nothing like the smell of freshly printed money. And begin to stick in your pocket. Because the closer that you get to that client. The more of this you are going to get. Because if you walk over and walk behind that client, put your hand on their shoulder and say to yourself, "Ha ha ha ha, their ass is mine." You will begin to adjust your attitude in a direction that moves towards success.

Now I want you to do another exercise. I want you to go into a group this time and I want you to make the same pitch, only this time, I want you to make your voice as sumptuous as you possibly can. I want you to stick in lots of ambiguities and I want you to make your pitch to somebody else in the group. Just switch it around a little bit. So that you're talking to another person. But yet, the others will still have the ability, and I want the other two people to stand behind you while you do, and to throw in suggestions. Not too many. Say things like, "Slow down." Somebody else can say, "Pace his breathing." Somebody else can throw out a nice ambiguity so that you can hear new voices in the back of your mind, telling you new things that you can try and do. When you finish this book, I want people to go, "How was the Persuasion Engineering™ book?" You can go, "It was better than sex."

Did you guys see that tv program where they have the hypnosis show, and everybody that comes out they go, "It was better than sex"? "How was it for you?" "It was better than sex." You see I want you hypnotize them and go, "It will make you successful, I will make four times the money in half the time and your orgasms will last four times as long, and be four times as intense." Oooooooo, you're getting it. I had somebody once who in their head goes "How? But I can't do it."

Did I ever tell you the Gazelle story? There are two lionesses, sitting out there and they are looking out and there is this pack of gazelle's going by and the one lioness goes, "I'm hungry," fffffft, runs up and grabs a gazelle and eats it. Great! Sits down next to the other lioness and the gazelles go by again and the other lioness goes, "Will you get me a gazelle?" And she goes, "Get your own fuckin' gazelle." And she goes, "But they're so fast. And I hurt my paw." And she goes, "Get your own fucking gazelle. And she goes, "Well, but I have a cold." Two months later, two hunters go out onto the tundra and they look and there is a dead lioness that starved to death. Don't let it be you, go do the exercise. Make it good, make it quick, and make it clean.

Now back to that list of objections I asked you to put together. Now, there has been a traditional view inside of most sales programs, most persuasion programs, that the trick is to overcome objections. And I've always found that to be kind of silly because if you do anything for any length of time, it seems like you should know what they're going to be ahead of time. And if you know what they are going to be ahead of time you should be able to find ways of inoculating so that you don't get them in the first place. If you have to overcome the same objections over and over again, that doesn't seem like planning to me. It's the same thing I find when people deal with stress. People always tell me that they want to reduce their stress, then I always tell them why have it in the first place. It seems to me that if you plan on having stress, if you have plan on having objections then you're a bad planner. Through the years one of the things that I've noticed very quickly is that there just aren't that many objections to anything. Now, what I'd like to do is, I'd like to take a few moments and go over a few that we've come across as some examples.

For example, people don't have enough time, (they are just about to die. Is that what they mean by that?) Haven't got enough time for health care? They don't have enough time to go to a chiropractor's office? Wouldn't that be easy to turn around? I haven't got enough time to go to the chiropractor's office (like I haven't got enough time to be healthy). And you go, "I understand. So, you'd rather be less efficient in everything that you do, by feeling bad?"

Or, they equate the amount of money they spend with whether or not they want healthcare. "That's good. Because after all who would want their sex life to be better? That wouldn't be worth anything, would it?"

If you wait until these things come around, people will bring them up. But if you know ideas make it so that things are, because "not everything is covered by your insurance. Not everything works either. You see, most insurance is for when things go wrong and you are in pain and get very sick. Do you know there are people that aren't willing to spend money to have their life be vibrant, they'd rather wait until they get sick. What idiots! Isn't that the craziest thing you've ever heard of? Now what was it you were going to say?"

Now, if you don't inoculate people against these things, they'll actually bring them up and say them to you. But worse than that, they will actually think them. The trick is, that if you know what objections are going to come up, if you can pre-inoculate, if you can take and put a frame around it and you can put a frame around anything. Look at the stuff that people are able to sell.

Listen to this: mobile homes. When you go on vacation a couple of weeks a year, why not bring everything you own with you. It's the world's most expensive way to travel third class. Now I know this because I always looked at people in these things and thought, this is a really nutty thing. But I got this idea, it was last year. I was doing a tour, and I was doing one in San Diego and one in Los Angeles and I thought, "You always leave the dog at home, why not rent a mobile home?" I don't know about you. You probably drive back and forth to work too much, but I've put, in the last four years, twelve thousand miles on my car, which means I don't drive very much. I drive about three thousand miles a year and that's about it. And when I drive, I drive in a very small place where you go very very fast up and down. But I saw an ad on TV, it just struck me, It was in the middle of the night, I was working on something, this guy came on and said, "We will rent you any mobile home." and for forty bucks a day. I thought, "Gee, that sounds so cheap. Maybe, I'll just slowly drive down and then I'll edge my way out. So I went over to this place and I rented this gigantic thing."

It was called a "Bounder". Good name for it. I went back to my house and loaded everything I own in it and proceeded to drive to San Diego. Now if you've never driven anything that's the size of a room, you shouldn't be allowed to. And that's all there is to it.

I must have given more people heart attacks than you can imagine. Because the part I was in was very small. And I just drove like that's all there was. I turned on the turn signal. But I used the Chinese method. Because I learned to drive in San Francisco, which is "turn on turn signal, count to three."

Now whether it's chiropractics and chiropractic medicine, you would think that in this day and age, that there would be enough of a calendar that these insurance companies would get it togeth-er. But I think that your lobby needs to do some serious work, especially in the US. because I mean you walk around and there is a lot of bent people with back pains and stuff and I mean you can give people drugs until you are blue in the face but it's not going to help. A friend of mine owns a sports medical clinic, which is our way of doing chiropractics for five times the price. And he actually has five or six chiropractors working there. What he did is, he got one doctor that . . . everybody that comes in, sees him and he writes prescriptions and they get the chiropractic stuff, they get massages, they can go in and exercise and, to attract peo-ple, to make sure that they did come in, he fills this place with the most beautiful women you have ever seen. I mean everywhere you turn there is some beautiful woman asking you if you want something. You know would you like a glass of juice, would you like a massage anytime you want, when you are under treatment in this place and there is like a line in this building. When I went in there the first time, it didn't strike me right away. But sudden-ly I noticed, and then I thought to myself, "How do they stay so nice in here?" And then I discovered that he had his own hair-dresser and makeup artist and that, literally, they go in in the morning and they doll everybody up in the place. The guys all look like they are Adonis, and suddenly you feel out of shape. I don't care who you are. A guy that I went in with is a football player from our local football team and this guy is in shape and his hands are so huge. And I was going to demonstrate to them . . . I do a lot of body work with people . . . and I was going to demonstrate to the people there how to work with wrists, because wrists are very complicated, there are more bones in your wrists and your ankles then just about anywhere. In fact, you have more than you have in all the rest of your body put together. And when I walked in this place and I was going around, I noticed that, here are these people and they were doing all these strange things with machines and stuff, and sounds catch me, by the way. And suddenly as I was walking along, I realized that, that room sounded like steel monkeys fucking. That's what it sounded like to me. I give sounds names that's how I remember them. And I turned around and I looked at this guy the football player, who is a little concerned, because he didn't know what he was in for, he just knew that his career depended on it . . . because when your job is to run very very fast and to catch the football . . . then every once in a while you come up with your wrist bent. And his wrist was in a lot of pain, and they've done some orthoscopic surgery, which is sneaky surgery, and they've done all of this work on this thing. And when they were done, his hand was messed up and it just wouldn't work. It was a very expensive way of getting it to hurt in a new direction and my way to do it is I just put things where they are now. Because not everybody conveniently has got the same body. The principal of rolphers is they put everything back where it belongs, but when you don't have everything, they don't know what to do. I get a tremendous amount of people who have phantom limb pain. They've had a limb or an arm, especially during the Vietnam war, which for whatever reason, that gets removed in an accident. And it's not there and it hurts. And this is a real problem for normal medical doctors. And people come in and they say, "It hurts here." Well it's all in your head but it doesn't feel like it's in your head. The nerves in their body are telling them that something exists where it isn't.

Now if you keep this in mind, one thing is, that I find that any objection you get in a sale is like phantom limb pain. You cut off something and it hurts where it's not. Part of your job is to be able to move through and to know where these things would come and to make sure that while you are packaging, 'cause to me it goes like this: to get their attention, establish enough rapport to know how they are organized, where their pictures are, where their belief system is, and then to begin to package what you know about your product so that it will go through their decision process first and number two, so that you can inoculate against any kind of objection.

Now, the one thing that you need to be able to do in order to do this is to have your sensory acuity so heightened that you can just really detect yes and no signals because you need to find out what objections they're gonna have.

So, one of the things I've found through the years is that it's very helpful to learn to be a crystal ball gazer. So what we are going to do is we are going to start out by making you members of the psychic hot line. But not the one that you call up, but the one that you visit. Now the thing is, that, if you remember just like when I told you that you could take your hand and move it from curved to flat. "Ffftt." Make a little sound like that. And you go "Fffttt" and you get a nice thing which allows you to lock. For example, I've had people say, "Now I don't want you to think about this." They come into a car lot and when you walk up to them, they go, "I'm just here looking." Well they weren't talking, yet. I knew that. But basically they are trying to elude to me, that they came in to look at cars, not to buy one. Now, I know better. If they wanted to look at cars, they are all over the road. They are everywhere, they are all over the damn place. Whizzing by, you can stand on a corner and see just about every kind of car there is. So if they come in to a car lot, I know that there is just enough of them that wants to buy a car that I can have my way with them. Now, the problem is that most people's decision strategies have things where they go back and forth, to try to find out if they've made a decision.

They'll go, "It looks like a good opportunity but I don't feel ready, yet." So that when you pace people you really have to remember to pace all of them because when people go, "Oh no, I'm just looking", I'll say to them, "But you feel that you really want it." And they go, "Yeah, but it looks so expensive." I've already reversed it. The trick is to get the kinesthetics on your side, 'cause they always win. Did you ever notice that? That's why people have such trouble dieting, you know. They go, "It looks awfully rich in calories, but I feel I want to stuff it in my body." Great advertisement, by the way for chocolate, this is an advertisement I saw, it's a billboard, shaped like a refrigerator, and the outside of the refrigerator is decorated with candy. It doesn't even say anything, but there is an arrow pointing straight down next to it and underneath it is a candy store. "Candied refrigerator, buy it." That's my kind of advertisement.

Now, the thing I want you to do, is I want you to hold one hand up and take the other one, then I want you to imagine between them a curved object. And I want you to take your hand and put it on there so that you can actually make the object real. Now when you take your crystal ball, the trick is to lower it down so that it's just below eye level 'cause remember it doesn't exist. Well, some people forget that and they look at it, like there is going to be something in it. The trick is not to hypnotize yourself here. The trick is that you are learning to do something with unconscious communication. Now, as you go through, what we are going to do is, we are going to start the thing about going to "Psychics For Sales". What I want you to do is to sit down with a partner and I want you to look at your crystal ball and I want you to go through, and remember, have your list down where you can see it and begin to package a presentation that says, "I see chiropractics in your future." And you go, "Oh, I see you have some concerns about chiropractics." And then I want you to start to go through a listing program: "Oh, it's becoming clearer and clearer now. Oh, I see you have some fear that it's going to be painful.

Many foolish people think that. People think, they think it's going to be more painful than the way that they live."

Bureaucracy, it's no wonder. Chiropractics works too well for it to be accepted by insurance companies. It would be too intelligent of a decision.

I have an insurance company come to me and say they wanted to run a test. They wanted to find out if my, and only my, certified Neuro-Linguistic Programmers, because they have tried others . . . they wanted to use them for working with people who were alcoholics.

Most places treat them and then when they let them out they get drunk again. This doesn't seem like a very good treatment program and then they have to spend more money. So we ran an experiment and I gave them the names of my certified practitioners and for five years or so they compared the results of my people verses other treatment programs. Now the result was so bent. This is how bent it was: that it didn't look like a legitimate statistic. That's what they told me. So we're not allowed to give insurance because we did too well. I said, "Well, you want us to go back and make some of them alcoholics again?" And he said it was too late. If we had done that earlier . . .

Anyway, once you have your crystal ball, what I want you to do is to begin to slowly go through your sales pitch and I want you to ham this up, play it up a little bit, but mostly I want you to concentrate, that if you do this, 'cause you can really do this with people. It's amazing you can say, for example, "I see in my crystal ball something in her future that has to do with sex." You start blushing already, they go, "Yeah, what is it?" It's wonderful, too. But it's so unorthodox. Now, and you know about it already. "Could it be," and then you begin to run through a listing program where you go, through these objections, you can say, "Oh you're afraid of chiropractics. So your major concern is that, that you won't be able to make the time, no no , is it about money? or it, it's unclear," and as you begin to go through . . . list the objections, you'll begin to notice that you get non verbal responses, that there are things that people respond to, more intensely than others. As soon as you locate one, and when you start getting it, these are the things to look for.

Now remember the peripheral part of your vision watches for movement. The phobic part of your vision is what you see with. So when you take a crystal ball, you always want to get it so that you put it in front of their eyes. Move it off to the side a little bit, so that you and they are looking at the same thing, but watch for movement with your peripheral vision. Now as you begin to play with this a little bit make a few jokes and stuff. I even do this kind of thing, like sometimes, I say "Now, I know that you want to buy a house and I'm not sure exactly what the things that you are looking for in a house are, I'd have to be a crystal ball gazer," and I literally go, "I'd have to have a crystal ball. Are you looking for two or three bedrooms?" You can go through and in a matter of moments elicit all the information that you need. Because, you'll get all the unconscious responses about what the characteristics are of what they want, and then simultaneously go through and find them, and then you go, "And I know that you are pretty worried about the price." Now, if you don't get a head nod on that one, I go, "Or else it really doesn't matter that much. Why, I have this place over here in such and such a space, it's a big house, it's a wonderful house, it's a house most other people, other than you wouldn't be able to afford, but now, inside your mind, there is another place . . ."

Now as you go through this each and everyone of those objections I want you to begin to build a frame for it, that makes it so that it's an idiotic thing to do, or else . . . and I want you to point out the characteristics about what makes it foolish. For example, if you were more efficient as a human being and felt better, you're going to make more money. And also some people think you have to go to a chiropractor for life because people are always talking about wanting to get adjustments and it's that when people start feeling better, they start wanting to do it more. It only takes a certain amount of time to get used to . . . to get you so you are really back on track. But you know, sometimes people find that it makes them feel so much better that they want even more. But I wouldn't be worried wanting to be too healthy, yet.

Let's just start at the beginning. The task is: build your crystal ball. Remember, whenever you want to create a curve surface, build one out so that you can see it. So that you have that texture. If you hallucinate it, it's much easier. And put it in the right place and say, "It'll be wonderful. More than you ever expected."

Isn't it nice to not be disappointed? It requires adequate planning. You have to think of something that will make you feel good, rather than when you feel bad. I always tell all my clients that disappointment requires adequate planning, so don't. Only plan for delight and that's what you'll find. Okay, now, make sure your objections in your own mind are concise . . . it should be things that you should write in a few words, not in a paragraph because your clients will be very distinct in whatever it is. They'll go "Well yeah, aren't people afraid to live in this neighborhood?" And I go, "Yes, some people are, but you know that was back in the fifties. They are all dead. Do you have a calendar by the way?"

Remember temporal predicates are one of the best ways to move a problem. Move it into the past. Move their hopes into the future, become clairvoyant. That is, learn to watch for unconscious cues because in them, you'll find the answers to how to avoid everything. Go forth.

Well I've had a bunch of people come in and seeing how much harder they could make this. What it is about human beings, and their ability to take the simple and make it complex? Only human beings can screw up fucking. I constantly get these calls, and the person that works for me comes up to me and goes, "Well he wants an appointment. But he wouldn't say what it is." Ummm, we know what it is.

If you let your natural processes as a human being . . . your ability to speak is hard wired. You don't have to look at pictures and know what to say. It doesn't come out good that way. And when you speak, listen to yourself. If you say the wrong thing change it. Remember the nice thing about words is they disappear just as you say them. You know the trick of trying to hold images in your mind is not the way to become clear as a human being. Although many individuals believe that. If you've got that kind of a theory, you would become so clear you had one picture, and you'd get stuck in it. And believe me, I've had many, many clients that are that way. The trick is to understand that there aren't good and bad things. There's a notion from psychology that people are broken and all this stuff. Get it out of your minds.

Realize that there is nothing wrong with being compulsive. You just want to make sure that you put the right things through the compulsion machine. I mean think of right now, every human being that exists has compulsions and has fetishes. Now, this is not good or bad, the problem is that they are sniffing shoes. The problem isn't that they want to do something all the time, the problem is what they put through the machine. The machine itself is lovely. What if you were compulsive about getting things done. Wouldn't that be nice? What if you had a fetish for cold calling. Now suddenly it doesn't sound so bad. You wouldn't go into a psychologist and go, "You know, hey man, I just have to make these calls and have to make more money all the time."

I tried an experiment one time, I had the unusual experience of running a friend's company when he got sick. He went to a foreign country, checked into a hotel and then was hospitalized within forty-eight hours. He got legionnaire's disease. By the way legionnaire's disease is completely curable. Don't you remember in Philadelphia all those guys from the American Legion went in this hotel, and they all died? Like thirty seven of them died in this hotel. Well it turns out that nobody had to die. The center for disease control goofed because when they always checked out bacteria to try to isolate diseases. What they do is they take samples and they put them in what amounts to a little oven, cook them up and when they multiply then they can see them. Well it turns out that legionnaire's disease is a mutant form of bacteria that lives and thrives in air conditioners. In other words, you would have to put it in the refrigerator to get it to multiply. And they never noticed anything like that.

I'm a firm believer in placebos. I think that placebos are a great thing. Every drug in the US is tested against placebos. That means we know a lot more about placebos than anything. But the FDA doesn't look at it that way, because you know, these are the people that say, "Let me look at that." (as they cover their face) Why do they have to cover their face? What, too much light gets in there, their ideas get blurry? I mean what's the story here? What happens here is that the people just aren't thinking. If placebos' work and you know, it's amazing the results they get with these things. For most things placebos will work eight out of ten times as good as something else. So I decided that one time to put a product out on the market called placebo. At the time Robert Dilts was my graduate student and I loved being a professor: you had slaves. It appealed to my inner nature . . . and we called them graduate students. Some of you were slaves and you know what I'm talking about.

But anyway, Robert came in and I said, "Robert, I want you to go down and I want you get all the studies that have been done, I want all the research of placebos for all the following things." And I had taken headaches and all the common household stuff. And then I put it all in a little book so what you got was a little bottle of empty gelatin capsules. I didn't even bother to put anything in them. These were just empty gelatin capsules and you'd look up and if you had a headache, you'd open it up and you'd read and find out that four out of five times placebos work as well as aspirin, so you would take six just to be safe. Well it worked for me. I tried it, it worked. You know, okay, and I'd take six of them and it would be gone. Well the FDA thought and went out and said I couldn't do this. I'm giving people nothing. "I'm sorry. Placebos. This is not going to work. So you can't do it."

I don't know if you've read the side of food containers. I read one the other day. You read this and some of these things sound like the contents of a bomb. There is like fifty six different things in a can of pudding. I mean my memory having made pudding from scratch was that it didn't take fifty things. And I said, "Well maybe they're food coloring and I looked at it, and I said if anybody deliberately tried to make it this color, they should be shot." It was butterscotch pudding, by the way." I mean it kind of looked more like something that should come out of somebody than go into them . . . anyway when my friend got sick, he had to leave the country because in order to get the kind of treatments that he wanted to get he had to go somewhere else.

He flew to Switzerland, and they did something that, according to the FDA in our country, hasn't been proven. However, now he doesn't have the disease. But of course that doesn't count, because it could have spontaneous remission. Whatever that means. I've had a lot of those in my career, by the way. We've used hypnosis to do all kinds of stuff and anytime I've done it, with any kind of cancerous substance whatsoever . . . I mean, we've done it where they've had X-rays . . . you can see there is this big thing and we used hypnosis and they would go back and it would be gone and they said, "Well yeah, but that was probably spontaneous remission." And I said, "Yeah, timely spontaneous remission."

Well while my friend was gone and I had his business, 'cause he asked me, "I have to leave and I have to leave tonight and I have the warning, and everybody that I know is a thief." And he said, "If I left my business to anybody else, they would run it into the ground. If you'll come and run it, I'll probably come back and be making more money than I ever did." And he said, "And I'm going to need a lot of it, 'cause this unproven procedure I am going to use, costs a lot of money." Not to mention the fact that going to Switzerland, always costs a lot of money. And if you've been there, and know what I'm talking about. A cup of coffee is $10, if you're not Swiss, by the way. If you are over there, learn to imitate the Swiss accent, at least, otherwise the price of everything quadruples. You didn't know that, but I've got news for you, you'll find out. The Swiss are prejudice against everyone. And for a price. It's not that they hate, they just charge for not being Swiss, right? Did you ever notice that the Swiss, have the largest denomination of bills? Right, you can't get a $1000 bill in America. But in Switzerland they are all over the place. We need them and they give them to tourists, so that we can buy things like coffee. And sweaters. And I've never seen a country like that, they have on every corner a pastry shop and a watch store and a chocolate store. Those of you who have been there, know what I am talking about. I mean every time you turn around they're constantly going, "Oh it's time for chocolate. Well, better have a pastry, you know." You'd think they would come in and go, "I'm Swiss." But they are not. Because they are too busy being in stress because they are on the stress diet. One of the most effective ones I know of.

Any of you ever had a terrible crisis go on and discover you lose weight? It's Richard's new stress diet, the one that I am using with people. I just put them in an absolute and utter stress. And they either die of a heart attack or lose weight. Works pretty good.

Anyway, when I had this business, it wasn't something that I was accustomed to. They sold women's lingerie, and they manufactured it and they didn't have stores or anything, at that time anyway. And at the time I was twenty three years old and I forgot to ask him, "What do you do?" 'cause he's somebody that I know, I had just gone diving with him. So I went down and I went into where the factory was. And he had this guy, he was sort of second in command and started showing me around and when I realized that what they sold was women's lingerie, I thought. "Hmmmm, a rare and unprecedented opportunity to find. . ." all they did was manufacture and then sell to stores and then, of course, the stores had to sell it before they would order more, which seemed very inefficient to me. What I thought about was dating . . . just popped right into my mind. I said, "Now, what if we could get guys to have a way of having lingerie to meet women." And this guy running this place looked at me and said, "Your nuts." And I said, "Yes, I am, and proud." I thought, "What if we could just have a way that people could just send us the money directly," and the guy said, "What do you mean?" I said, "it's called a catalog." And this was a long time ago. Now they have catalogs for everything.

It struck me, that, if you were going to sell lingerie, maybe you should use women. And it just popped into my mind. I don't know why. But anyway, he had a sales force, he had five guys and they went around to stores and they went in and they'd get these buyers at the department stores to buy some stuff. But anyway, we tried taking pictures of all the things and gave some description and put it in a catalog and then I started a program by which people could have, because I believe in the concept of having more than one business, that people could take the catalogs, they could go out, pass them out and then if people ordered off of that, and had their insignia that was actually printed into the catalog and they would just get a check in the mail. So if I walked up to you on the street and handed you a catalog, and you ordered out of it then, I would get a check.

So then I took a bunch of people and I said, "Look this is a rare and unprecedented opportunity for you, in your spare time, to constantly make money." You could mail them out if you wanted to. I didn't care what they did. And what a great way to meet people. At the time I had this thing called the flirting class. But we just did that as a lark just for fun. When I taught the flirting class, what I discovered is that there are some people that don't know how to say "Hello". Now this is why we want to begin to build new fetishes. Those of you who cold call on the phone, and those of you who prospecting for whatever it is, think about it. When you drive down the road as a chiropractor, you look at all those bent and broken people, every building is just full of people that can't even get up that well. Think about all of the insurance companies that are carrying heavy loads of people on disability. I don't know about you, if I got paid to be injured, my body would probably hurt like hell. The problem is, you can't get any insurance company to pay you as much as I make for being broken.

Most people don't know that feeling good is better than feeling bad, because they're not any good at feeling good. Now, the concept that I want to get across to you is, I know every single person reading this has got a fetish. I'm not crystal ball gazing, am I. And I know for some of you it's very intense. Now if you could take the feeling you had for example, chocolate. When I say that, I look around and you should, too. I'm crystal ball gazing. When you are, look around a little bit.

Stop and think, how many people will see, Godiva chocolates? I don't like chocolate, but there are people, who, when you say the word "Godiva" everything in their sole goes wild. The reason I am saying that is to find out who they are. Now, because I'm not really looking for somebody who wants to sniff shoes, but we are just trying to find something that we can convert to something else.

The trick is, we are looking for the fetishes. You remember you are reading this to learn things. You know the stuff between your ears? There is a purpose why that thing is there: it's called thinking. I want you to use it to concentrate on what we are doing here. Don't think about the candy and the lingerie, think about the training that's behind it. Or . . . can be done.

It's a great line "can be done". People say, "Well, I have a problem like that." And you go, "Can be done." Instead of if they go, "Oh, what a beautiful car." And you go, "Just." And that's a very important word, just. Keep it in mind. It means only. Let's see, just keep that thought.

You know that little exercise you did with the submodalities earlier? You went through and you found out about the difference between the strong belief and something that was not a strong belief. Now, we are going to do that again, only this time, what we are going to do is a little different. You can do this content free so that you get something good. Get yourself a partner and I want you to have that person think of something for which they have an absolute and overwhelming fetish. They have to have it, they have to do it. They are compulsed. When they even think about it they should glow. If they don't glow have them pick something else.

Now, I want you to have them think of the thing they have the fetish for and then I want you to also ask them, where they would like to have a compulsion. Do they not cold call enough? We want to build in a driving, pulsing force in you that gets you to be successful. It's not enough to have skills to know what to do. You have to become carnivorous. What I did was, I installed in this friend's of mine business, I took all the people and I sat them down and I gave everyone of them, no matter what they did, the guy who worked the warehouse, the accountant, even the tele-marketers I gave them a compulsion to cold call.

The guy in the warehouse said that in spare minutes, he would go over to the pay phone and call people. Why not? It was like, "Gee could I have a few minutes off to go out and use the tele-phone, man?" "I thought of a few more people I could call and send catalogs to, man." And I said, "Well, I don't know, maybe ten minutes, but make it fast, ten minutes, man, how many calls can you make in ten minutes?" "Oh, man I can make like fifty calls in like ten minutes, man." "Hey, there's somebody on the phone, get off the phone. It's my pay phone, get away from the phone, no, no it's mine, mine, mine."

I installed a lot of pay phones. I made money off that, too. See, multiple businesses, you've got to get them going, get them coming, get them from every direction.

I made every single person at the company a marketing agent. Everybody, now, can make commissions at the company, even people who don't work there can make commissions. I now have a vehicle to build and then it struck me. I wanted to have the biggest sales force that any company has ever had. So, I went to the Boy Scouts of America. However, they didn't like my idea. But we did come up with something for them, but I thought you know, they are always coming by selling candies, selling something. What if they came by and sold something that you really wanted.

I said, "There's a half a million people in Future Farmers of America." Members, these are 14 year-old boys by the way, 14 year-old girls who need money to pay for their cow or whatever it is. So they come by and they sell . . . you know, it's a guilt sale .

. . one of those. They go, "Well, my son needs to go to camp, you know, can you buy some candy bars?" You know this one? Well if they come by and they want to sell you some junky candy or some tickets to some game you won't go buy. But think about it, if they came by and offered you a teddy? That would be different, wouldn't it? They'd say, "I'm selling these teddy's, look in this catalog you can have anything." Sexy brochures, you know. Not only would they be making more money for their projects, but they would be getting a future education. I thought it was a good idea.

Anyway, we had to give them something else to sell. We actually gave them books on agriculture. But I kept looking, "where could I find a group of people to do this?" And I discovered, it was so simple: college. I sent my guys up to college, they would go in and they'd go, "Who needs extra money?" You're starting to notice these rhetorical questions. "Is there somebody here that needs some extra money?" "You. Feeling a little poor today are we?"

Now, the thing that I want you to do is I want you to illicit and this time it's with an "I". Illicit a response, with an "I". Don't sound it out, man it won't help. Finetics, F let's see F fafafa, what word is that pohonics, pa pa pa honics. What a stupid system that is. Good, sound out the word angiogram and by the time you get to the end of the word, you'll need one. Now, what I want you to do is to go through and get all the summages, mark down, don't make this into a big thing. Just on your list, mark down only the things that are different between the way they experience. For example, if you have somebody who, in their business, if they would make a lot more money . . . this is the question, "What would you like to be compulsive to do and it would make sure that you made a lot more money?" If you looked at a telephone and had to cold call . . . if every time a new prospect was there, you walked across the room . . . because a lot of people, when they see a customer walk in, it's like gravity gets heavy and it's like that dating thing . . . the hardest part was getting these guys to walk over and say hello. I used to actually take them in a course, it's not on video, but when I taught the flirting course, I would take thirty guys to a shopping mall because . . . I don't know why they go to bars, there aren't any good women in bars, they're all in the shopping malls. If you want to find good women, go to Neman Markus. And they are all over the place. And they are in a heightened state of awareness where they feel really good.

And then just go stand in the jewelry department. And they'll walk up and they'll go, "Do you work here?" and you'll go, "No, but I can help you." And then you look at them and you go, "Do you want to feel really good?" When they go in these malls they are like the great white hunters. They are just like stalking that sale. It's really something. You could select them by departments, stores every thing. You go, "What am I in the mood for, today? Designer, I want a designer woman . . . let's see, so I will go up to that second story and go into that" . . . you know you can even pick their economic levels . . . everything. When you want a woman who will buy you presents, you go into this department, and when you are feeling generous you go into that department. Ummmmm.

It's just getting your brains to think about prospecting it's just a metaphor for . . . I'm a hypnotist remember? But there isn't any metaphor like a true metaphor, is there? 'Cause there are some guys in there right now, "Go in the mall, pick up chicks" . . . "and then if you want chicks to buy you presents, you go to the designer thing and I never feel generous so we won't write that down . . ."

The other great place too, is those haircutting salons. I, like you just wander into those places, and sit down and stare at somebody while they are having their hair cut or while they are having a dye or something. They'll go, "What are you looking at?" And then you go, "You look so beautiful." 'cause that's why they are there. They call that pacing . . . Richard style. And then you say to them, "Are you going to be free after this?" What no, they are going to go to jail? Don't ask them if they are going to go somewhere, if you just ask if they are going to be free and then tell them where to meet you. You see, don't bring up objections and you won't get them. I know some of you guys, I've heard the shit that you say, it's so terrible and it embarrasses them so. Oh, I heard one the other night, let's see, this guy walks up to this woman, this has got to be the worst line, and he goes, "So, uh, babe, what are you here for?" What the fuck does that mean? I don't even know what that means. "Hey, babe what are you here for?"

I noticed on the side of somebody's video tape once, they had a tape they made about not smoking, that if you look at it, it says (No. 1), I know they want it to say "Number one." But if the unconscious remembers analog, it comes out "No one." So if you have no one smoking tape, then the unconscious is going to look at it from the side and go, "Couldn't be for me, because it's not for any one." So maybe we'll be changing the title of that. There's a lot of times, people think something is going to have one meaning and it has another, and the trick is, are you interested in pride or cash? And my thing is, I'll take the cash, fuck the pride.

Now what I want you do to is to get yourself a partner, and when you have the partner, I want you to go through and when you have all the submodalities of the thing they have a fetish for, then what I want you to do is to take the thing they want, and I want you to go, "Fffffttt" and pull it up inside, the same location, make it the same size and the same distance all the things that constitute . . . and you will discover suddenly, you have a fetish for it. Now, then have them close their eyes and I want you to double the size of the image. And I want you to give them, a kick ass post hypnotic suggestion. It says that every time they see this they are going to drool and that's going to just force them to quadruple their income.

Money is the root of all evil. So let's get down to the root of the matter. See, it doesn't say that it is evil, it just says that it is the root. So as long as we keep the roots clipped everything will be fine. We can dry those roots out and make tea out of it. And then tell people, who make those kinds of metaphors . . . to wait. The rest of you get to it, now.

(Demonstration subject) Well let's see here. Come here Ted, come up here. Just sit down, right here. Take this (pen) and you don't need this (his book), just sign right there. That's how you get them to close. You can go now, Ted. If you can't give commands by that time, you haven't paced the shit out of them, that's all that I can say. I find that as, I call it the pen interrupt pattern, which is done this way. (Still demonstrating) Yeah, you, too, your soul is mine. You touched the pen.

See I always find at that point in time, that something that uplifts a little bit, I throw them the pen, roll it off the end of the clip board. Whatever it is, something that gets them to respond physically. Remember, if you give them too much time, at that point in time, people have been trained all over the world that when you hand them the contract, to have a bad feeling. Jump over it. A lot of times, people say, "Well I should read this." And you go, "Well you'll have a copy at home." That's the best time to do it. By that time they should already know the details.

People would say, "What about financing?" And I'd go, "Your credit is good with me, we'll work that out later" because after all, if they don't have credit then we won't give them the car, right? But after all it shouldn't be a painful process.

I've always thought it was an amazing thing that you could go out and buy a shirt for fifty bucks and feel better. You go out and buy a car, and you feel worse because of the process that you're put through, in most of this stuff. And most of it is analog, because the people who are doing the selling start to get a feeling, that something is going to go wrong, so they induce it. That's what happens.

Buying a house, this is one of the amazing things. They go, "Give us a check for $1000 and we can get you into escrow and then we'll begin . . ." and I like this "the long process of escrow." It already sounds like it has weight on it. You shouldn't feel that. See when I do it, the minute they sign you want to go, "Oh boy, how exciting! Congratulations!", because the more you put that congratulations on the end of it, the more you become uplifted. Then there is another thing which I do, is I'll stop and I'll look at them and I'll take the contract and I'll go, "I changed my mind" and I'll grab a hold of the edge of it and start to tear it up because I always want to make a check to make sure that I am not going to get any buyer's remorse. It is amazing the minute you go to tear up the contract they go, "Huh, what are you doing?" And I'll stop and I'll say, "Well look, let me put it this way, are you sure, that this is the right thing?" And they'll go, "Yeah." And I'll go, "because you have to be absolutely sure, sure enough that you are going to tell everyone you know."

And I'll tell you one of the toughest sales that people have to make is door to door sales, because for some reason people have become suspicious of this process, anyway. I worked for a company called Celebrity China. And they sell China door to door. And this is a tough sale. Because they have to overcome every stigmatism there is. In the US they have a law which says people have 72 hours to change their mind. Now, if you have 72 hours to change your mind, most of the time the people wouldn't if it weren't for their friends and loved ones. People would do this, they'd go, "You bought china from a door to door salesman?" Now to begin, with the china was beautiful. Actually, it was because every meal that we had was on different china and china breaks.

There is nothing like unnerving people. They have these beautiful crystal glasses. I kept taking them and tapping them on things and finding if they would shatter. I wanted to know. Because I had bought china one time and beautiful crystal. But then I had kids. Now, I learned, I spent ten years in the melmac club. And I wanted to find something a little heartier but, anyway we had beautiful crystallabra things, like you guys would be sitting there now, they had little tables in front of you and you had a beautiful thing stuffed in noshuan and crystal. Great idea for a conference. We nibbled our way through for three days. Bit by bit, piece by piece.

But anyway, they all told me that the toughest thing was, that they didn't know how to deal with this. So, when I told them, I said, "Me, I always start to rip the contract and when you look at people and you say, look if you're absolutely sure, because one of the things you need to do is to future pace or inoculate and protect people against buyer's remorse." Because most of the time it is induced by other people. Cause they would be real excited and they would tell somebody, "I bought this china from this guy that came by from the door." And people go, "What?" They go, "You bought china from a door to door salesman?" You must have been ripped off. Now, these guys said, "How can we avoid it?" And I said, "Don't." I said, "Before you go and you hold up the contract and you start you go, "Your not ready for this." And people go, "Wait, what do you mean, I'm not ready." And I go, "Don't you know what's going to happen?" I said, "It's going to be your sister, it's going to be your brother, it's going to be your uncle, it's going to be your next door neighbor, you feel good now, don't you?" And they'll go, "Yeah." And I go, "Would you let anybody steal your good feelings?" I said, "Every time, you see this brochure here, I want you to feel this wonderful. Every time you look at your table set with beautiful china and crystal, I want you to feel wonderful. I want to know for sure that you feel better than you feel right now, do you understand?" And people go, "Yes." And I go, "Well, people are going to come in and say, "Oh, but it's the wrong pattern." And I always exaggerate it. I use what I refer to as the synthetic twerp phenomenon. Because that's what these people are when somebody comes into your house and goes, "Oh, but you paid too much but blah blah blah . . ." And I imitate them and I go, "And if you can let any one of those people get to you, if you're not ready to look at them and just laugh, because they just want to deprive you of your happiness . . .". I say, "Are you sure enough in your conviction that you have now . . . cause otherwise I'll rip this up and go sell it to someone who deserves it."

You're getting into this, aren't you? Well it's the only way I feel that you can really protect people, when they drive up with a new car and they go, "You bought a Chrysler?" Give me a break. Let alone people coming home in a Mercedes they go, "Boy, they must have seen you coming." And every line that I know . . . well, they didn't see you, they lured you. To me it was like fishing. I even brought a fishing pole to work. Put a sign on it. And said "Enter Here." Put it out on the street and you know people turned in. They had a sign inside their head. It said, "Help me." You see people are not good at buying themselves presents. People aren't good at things, like if you sell insurance. Insurance, is a wonderful thing but it's no good, if it doesn't give you what it's really supposed to, which is peace of mind. How many of you have rented a car at the airport and they ask you would you like the insurance and I say, "What does the insurance get you?" And that means, "if there is any damage to the car whatsoever, you don't have to worry." And I thought, "What a great thing. I can go out and smash this fucker all up." Hey, you know, the next time you feel kind of frustrated and stuff you know, go down to the airport, rent a car for the afternoon, pay the ten bucks, you can bang it off of walls, everything. I turned in one one time, that there wasn't even a panel left on the thing, that didn't have dings in it. The front was smashed in, the side was gouged out and when I pulled up the guy said, "What happened?" And I said, "I don't know, I pulled into a Seven Eleven and I came out and it was like this." It was a great thing. We actually used to go and rent them in pairs and have demolition derby's with them. Sixteen cars at Avis and I thought they were going to be all over my ass, because I got carried away that week. And I got a big package like this, from Avis in the mail. And I thought, "Oh shit, they are going to sue me or something." And I opened it up and you know, Avis gave me a credit card. They said, we like this guy, he rents lots of cars. Sometimes two and three at a time. Sometimes we never even left the parking lot. We just smashed them up right there. But see, if you have the right attitude about what a product provides, what a service provides . . . look, I want you to know that when you bought insurance, you bought what you buy as a sense of security that you don't have to worry that if you buy renter's insurance in your own apartment, you walked out . . . You should turn around and look at the door and go, "It doesn't matter who steals anything. I get a new one." What a great deal.

We have phenomenal things available to us in this country. The fact that you could literally go out and buy a better body without exercise. It's very cool, you go in and people just move the bones around and make you feel better. You can go out and buy massages.

I don't know about you but I don't like the idea of having to go out and hunt down animals everyday and shoot them or digging up roots. I think the supermarket's the coolest thing around. And as you go by, oh we'll have a little slice of cow. A little slice of lamb. Oh, how about a bird that flew through the air, and a fish in the sea. To me, one of the things that people who are in the business of selling and in the business of persuasion need to understand is that the whole process is a wonderful thing. The fact that human beings have so much trouble over all, running their brains, they need us. So that they can enjoy the process of being a wanton consumer. I don't know about you, I have people who actually get mad 'cause they get catalogs in the mail. Not me. I go through each and every one, and I go, "Oh, that would feel good, ummmm, ahhhhhh, ummmmm."

And people need to be taught to enjoy the generation that we live in. Because I have noticed that the people who do not spend money do not make money. You know those people who are always saving every dime. They are always broke. Now, I don't know where it goes, but it goes to something else. Plus they never know how to use money and enjoy it. They might as well not make it. If your ability to realize that you can make it, especially in the free societies that we live in . . . Just think we could be living where . . . who are these people? Do you realize that So Damn Insane was elected? Who did he run against, Completely Insane? "Yes, we'll vote for So Damn Insane, we don't want Completely Insane as our leader, then there's Totally Insane." To me, people like that need to be taught a lesson, and I don't think it was done. I think that the fact that people want to reelect people like that. Instead we should be buying them presents. Like a six by six condo. You know what that is? It's a mausoleum. I always hear that song, "There is a place for him" and I always think of that guy, every time. I have pictures of how much good he can do for the world when he ain't around no more. Because it takes a lot of education for a society to be a capitalistic society.

Our government, they want to take healthcare and turn it over to the same people that run the post office. I mean, I don't know about you, but in our country our post office doesn't work all that well. Plus every few years there is someone up in the tower with a rifle who used to work there. I don't know what we put on our stamps in our country. But it is really getting to be a problem. That out of these psycho's that go out on random shooting sprees in the US, seven out of ten of them worked at the post office. I don't know what it is about the post office but I don't go there anymore. I don't need to be pushed any harder.

I think the thing that I did when they had the presidential election, I voted no. Because I think it just encourages them if you elect them to office.

Now the thing is when you go to close and you should constantly be testing for this. I start right out, sometimes people walk in and they look at something and I go, "Wonderful isn't it? How are you going to pay for it? Credit card?" I say, "Give me your wallet." Do you know people hand it to you. It always amazed me. I don't even work in the store sometimes. I'm just there practicing, you know, and I go, "Give me your wallet." And I'll go through and I'll go, "Amex, that's the way to pay for it." And then they'll go, "Uh well, uh my Amex card isn't good anymore." "Well, let's go through here, what else you got? You've got Visa, Master Card." What a great thing: Master card. It sounds like something the Germans would have come up with, doesn't it. "I can pay for anything I have zee Mastercard."

To me, as long as you go through and you constantly test for close and you attach good feelings, it's really easy.

CHAPTER EIGHT

PRECISION PERSUASION ENGINEERING™

Now after you've done the exercises, I want you to stop and close your eyes, run back into where you came and started here in the beginning and begin to run through your mind, all the new things that you got to try. Because you want to connect all this with your real life. And I want your unconscious at the same time to begin to sort and search to find and feel all the opportunities that will be arising for you to do things in new ways so that you can find life somewhat better. Just think, it's Saturday night, now where could you use persuasion techniques on a Saturday night, I stop and I ask yourself inside your mind, "What would be a rare and unprecedented opportunity to begin to have new experiences? To make things feel better, to have new opportunities that are spread right out in front of you?"

Now if you looked at Saturday night in a new way, it's just a chance to begin to take the skills that you learned and to install them at the unconscious level, to begin to do things and new ways to find new things happening, then you will. If you don't, then you won't. Don't close the book and leave the learning behind. Realize that it's only the beginning of what you are going to do with the rest of your life.

And we want the rest of your life to be quite exciting. And we want you to begin to master yourself and master each and every opportunity to do things in new ways. As you are walking along and you hear people talking, when you hear a great ambiguity I want you to go, "Oohhh, I could use that." Maybe drop into a few stores tonight and see how shitty people really are at selling things. Maybe sell something, even where you don't work. Maybe you could go up and play the role of one of your clients, that's very tough and find out somebody else will do it.

The world is your learning laboratory.

I noticed when I ask the question, a fair number of you are single. And remember sex can kill you now, if you are not careful. It's not like the 60's, so I want you to experiment but experiment with protection and realize that you can take things in new directions if you catch my drift and my thrust. Because if you thrust into new areas and new ways, you may find that things are a lot easier. That, when you bathe people in tonality, that when you first concentrate on your nose, your throat, your chest and then get to that area by which, you can resonate it . . . spend a little time when you are in the shower, speaking and listening. You can hear yourself perfectly there.

Learn to hear what your tone of voice sounds like and to increase your range. Give yourself the ability to realize the more that you can let your tonality go "uuuup" and "dooowwwn" the more variations that you can have in tempo, the more you can control your syntax and embed questions and know when to anchor.

Wouldn't it be nice to know when to anchor? For example, one of my favorite questions boils down to this, "How do you know when you want to be seduced?" If you don't know, the answer to that question is it would be very hard to do things. And if somebody stops and you see their eyes move up, anchor it, say, "Excuse me a minute," and as they look at you go, " 'cause you like me. Wouldn't want to do anything exciting, foolish, something that might take you in whole new directions." And tonight while you sleep and dream I want the unconscious portion of each of you because it's been here and it's been close enough to hear. To realize that it's been learning a lot as well. You see if you package information in just the right way, a lot of it goes into the conscious but your unconscious can learn so much faster. And I wanted to begin to sort and search to the learning of the essence inside yourself because this particular book doesn't need these learnings.

You need to make sure that everything that each of both of you has learned here, begins to develop so that while you sleep and dream I want you to run unconsciously scenario after scenario. Because in your dreams time means nothing at all. You dream a week in a minute, a day in a second, so you can begin to run hundreds of thousands of scenarios so that it begins to feel familiar, to do things in new ways, to begin to make changes that will stay with you for the rest of your life and make every day a payday in excitement, cash. Because we still have much to do. You have to quadruple that income and do it in half the time. And you have to take that slow time at the bank where things seem to take forever and experience your orgasms just that way. You see it's not the bank that makes time go slow, it's your mind, that knows how to alter time. So while you are altering time inside your dreams, while you're moving as Einstein did on a beam of light, remember each new idea is capable of changing everything. And it's not that you want to change everything. So carefully select unconsciously, those things that don't suit you anymore. You don't need any more knots in your gut. You can adjust those backwards . . . untie them, and then open up to a whole new way. Find yourself doing more things that are more exciting and get to it. It's time to get out there in the world and boogie on down.

You can't get a degree in sales, you can't get a degree in persuasion, you can get a degree in important stuff, like Greek history. Yeah, poetry, Greek history. How about blatant. A language not spoken anywhere. Listen to this, I had a counselor, this counselor is sitting there and looking at me and she's dressed . . . she must have weighted about 370 pounds just to start with . . . she had on a blue and white polka dotted dress, the image is burned in my mind . . . and white socks, of all things. Her hair looked like she made it up in a Waring blender and she looks at my file and she goes, "Mr. Bandler, I noticed you haven't got a single class in Latin," and I said, "Well everyone that speaks Latin is dead, except for a few priests and I'm afraid to be around them. I said, "I don't go out with guys that where dresses." And she said, "This is not a laughing matter." And I went, "Don't you bet on it." She said, "Without three years of latin, how do you expect to be able to learn a language?" And I said, "When I was born, I didn't have any latin, I didn't have any languages, and I learned the language, I have a machine in my head that does that." The only institution I know capable of preventing you from learning the language is the school system. How many of you went to school, learned a language and don't know anything about it? It's phenomenal. Only a school system could do that. You know, you take anybody and just stick them in a country and they will end up learning the language, except for our president, who by the way spent a year in Russia. What the hell was he doing in Russia? What, going over there and finding out that it is the Mexico of Europe? I'm a kid, I grew up hiding under desks, for fear the Russians were going to blow us up. It turns out they can't even make an IC chip. They can't. They had to steal them from us. And of course, we gave them just the ones that we wanted to. It's ridiculous.

However, they are very good at sitting in outer space. That's what they are, They are very good at sitting in outer space. They can sit in outer space longer than anyone. Boy that scares me. So what I'm really afraid of is somebody who can hide in the dark.

So I decided, we should make our college.

◟ *GLOSSARY OF NLP TERMS*

Accessing Cues

Subtle behaviors that will both help to trigger and indicate which representational system a person is using to think with. Typical types of accessing cues include eye movements, voice tone, tempo, body posture, gestures, and breathing patterns.

Anchoring

The process of associating an internal response with some external trigger (similar to classical conditioning) so that the response may be quickly, and sometimes covertly, reaccessed.

Auditory

Relating to hearing or the sense of hearing.

Behavior

The specific physical actions and reactions through which we interact with the people and environment around us.

Behavioral Flexibility

The ability to vary one's own behavior in order to elicit or secure a response from another person.

Calibration

The process of learning to read another person's unconscious, nonverbal responses in an ongoing interaction by pairing observable behavioral cues with a specific internal response.

Calibrated Loop

Unconscious pattern of communication in behavioral cues of one person trigger specific responses from another person in an ongoing interaction.

Chunking

Organizing or breaking down some experience into bigger or smaller pieces. Chunking up involves moving to a larger, more abstract level of information. Chunking down involves moving to a more specific and concrete level of information. Chunking laterally involves finding other examples at the same level of information.

Congruence

When all of a person's internal beliefs, strategies, and behaviors are fully in agreement and oriented toward securing a desired outcome.

Context

The framework surrounding a particular event. This framework will often determine how a particular experience or event is interpreted.

Criteria

The values or standards a person uses to make decisions and judgments.

Deep Structure

Complete representation of the logical semantic relations in a sentence.

Four Tuple (or 4-tuple)

A method used to notate the structure of any particular experience. The concept of the four tuple maintains that any experience must be composed of some combination of the four primary representational classes: A,V,K,O – where A = Auditory, V = Visual, K = Kinesthetic, and O = Olfactory/ Gustatory.

Future Pacing

The process of mentally rehearsing oneself through some future situation in order to help ensure that the desired behavior will occur naturally and automatically.

Gustatory

Relating to the sense of taste.

Installation

The process of facilitating the acquisition of a new strategy or behavior. A new strategy may be installed through any of the NLP™ skills or techniques and/or any combination thereof.

Kinesthetic

Relating to body sensations. In NLP the term kinesthetics is used to encompass all kinds of feelings including tactile, visceral, and emotional.

Meta Model

A model developed by John Grinder and Richard Bandler that defines syntatic environments by which one can detect and challenge deletions, generalizations and distortions.

Meta Program

A process by which one sorts through multiple generalizations simultaneously as such Meta Programs control how and when. A person will engage in any set of strategies in a given context.

Metaphor

Stories, parables, and analogies.

Modeling

The act of creating a calculus which describes a given system.

Neuro-Linguistic Programming (NLP)

The study of the structure of subjective experience and what can be calculated from that.

Olfactory

Relating to smell or the sense of smell.

Outcomes

Goals or desired states that a person or organization aspires to achieve.

Pacing

A method used by communicators to quickly establish rapport by matching certain aspects of their behavior to those of the person with whom they are communicating - matching or mirroring of behavior.

Parts

A metaphorical way of talking about independent programs and strategies of behavior.

Predicates

Process words (like verbs, adverbs, and adjectives) that a person selects to describe a subject. Predicates are used in NLP to identify which representational system a person is using to process information.

Rapport

The presence of trust, harmony, and cooperation in a relationship.

Representational Systems

The five senses: seeing, hearing, touching (feeling), smelling and tasting.

Representational System Primacy

The systematic use of one sense over the others to process and organize in a given context.

Secondary Gain

Where some seemingly negative or problematic behavior actually carries out some positive function at some other level. For example, smoking may help a person to relax or help them fit a particular self-image.

State

The total ongoing mental and physical conditions from which a person is acting.

Strategy

A set of explicit mental and behavioral steps used to achieve a specific outcome.

Sub-Modalities

The special sensory qualities perceived by each of the five senses. For example, visual sub-modalities include color, shape, movement, brightness, depth, etc., auditory submodalities include volume, pitch, tempo, etc., and kinesthetic submodalities include pressure, temperature, texture, location, etc.

Surface Structure

An utterance.

Synesthesia

The process of overlap between representational systems, characterized by phenomena like see-feel circuits, in which a person derives feelings from what they see, and hear-feel circuits, in which a person gets feelings from what they hear. Any two sensory modalities may be linked together.

T.O.T.E.

Developed by Miller, Galanter and Pibram, the term stands for the sequence Test-Operate-Test-Exit, which describes the basic feedback loop used to guide all behavior.

Transderivational Search

The act of locating through meaning(s) which may not be explicit or implicit in a surface structure.

Translating

Connecting the meaning of one representation to the same meaning in another representation.

Visual

Relating to sight or the sense of sight.

Well-Formedness Conditions

In NLP, a particular outcome is well-formed when it is: (1) stated in positives, (2) initiated and maintained by the individual, (3) ecological – maintains the quality of all rapport systems, and (4) testable in experience – sensory based.

ADDENDA

SUBMODALITY COMPARISONS

VISUAL

Number of Images	_____	_____
Motion/Still	_____	_____
Color/B&W	_____	_____
Bright/Dim	_____	_____
Focused/Unfocused	_____	_____
Bordered/Borderless	_____	_____
Associated/Dissociated	_____	_____
Center Weighted/Wide Angle	_____	_____
Size (Relative to Life)	_____	_____
Shape	_____	_____
Three Dimensional/Flat	_____	_____
Close/Distant	_____	_____
Location in Space/Panoramic	_____	_____

AUDITORY

Numbers of Sounds/Sources	_____	_____
Volume	_____	_____
Tone	_____	_____
Tempo	_____	_____
Pitch	_____	_____
Pace	_____	_____
Timbre	_____	_____
Duration	_____	
Intensity	_____	_____
Direction	_____	_____
Rhythm	_____	_____
Harmony	_____	_____
More in one ear than another	_____	_____

KINESTHETIC

Location in body   _____   _____

Breathing Rate   _____   _____

Pulse Rate   _____   _____

Skin Temperature   _____   _____

Weight   _____   _____

Pressure   _____   _____

Intensity   _____   _____

Tactile Sensations   _____   _____

OLFACTORY & GUSTATORY

Sweet   _____   _____

Sour   _____   _____

Salt   _____   _____

Bitter   _____   _____

Aroma   _____   _____

Fragrance   _____   _____

Essence   _____   _____

Pungence   _____   _____

MILTON MODEL

The first set of language patterns is
the inverse of the

META MODEL™

The additional other important
language patterns include:

PRESUPPOSITIONS

INDIRECT
ELICITATION PATTERNS

PATTERNS IN
METAPHOR

MILTON MODEL
INDIRECT ELICITATION PATTERNS

Embedded Commands:
Embed directives within a larger sentence structure. "You can begin to *relax*"

Analogue Marking:
Set the directive apart from the rest of the sentence with some nonverbal analogue behavior

Embedded Questions:
Embed questions within a larger sentence structure. "I'm wondering what time it is."

Negative Commands:
Stating what you do want to occur and preceding this statement with the word "don't."

Conversational Postulates:
Yes/no questions that typically elicit a response rather than a literal answer: "Do you know what time it is?"

MILTON MODEL
PRESUPPOSITIONS

Subordinate Clauses of Time:
Before, after, during, as, since, prior, when, while, etc.

Ordinal Numerals:
Another, first, second, third, etc.

Use of "Or":
The word "or" between the given choices.

Awareness Predicates:
Know, aware, realize, notice, etc.

Adverbs & Adjectives:
Deeply, easily, curious about, etc.

Change of Time Verbs & Adverbs:
Begin, end, stop, start, continue, proceed, already yet, still, anymore, etc.

Commentary Adjectives & Adverbs:
Fortunately, luckily, innocently, happily, etc.

MILTON MODEL
INDIRECT
ELICITATION PATTERNS
AMBIGUITIES

Phonological Ambiguity:
Words that sound alike but have different meanings. I, eye; write, right, rite; weight, wait; their, they're, there; red, read, etc.

Syntactic Ambiguity:
Take a transitive verb, add "ing" after it, and place it before a noun. "They were milking cows."

Scope Ambiguity:
Occurs when it is unclear how much of the sentence an adjective, verb, or adverb applies to. "They went with the charming men and women."

Punctuation Ambiguity:
Put two sentences together that end and begin with the same word. "I'm speaking clearly to make sure that you can *hear* you are, in the process of..."

MILTON MODEL
PATTERNS IN
METAPHOR

Selection Restriction Violations:
The attribution of qualities to something or someone which by definition could not possess those
qualities. "The rock is sad."

Quotes:
Making any statement you want to make to another person as if you are reporting in quotes what
someone else said at another time and place.

META MODEL™

DELETION, DISTORTION, GENERALIZATION

and the Linguistic Patterns of Information Gathering

Wellformedness Conditions for Surface Structures:

1. Are well formed in English, and
2. Contain no transformational deletions or unexplored deletions in the portion of the model in which the person has no choice;
3. Contain no nominalizations (process is transformed into an event);
4. Contain no words or phrases lacking referential indexes;
5. Contain no verbs incompletely specified;
6. contain no unexplored presuppositions i the portion of the model in which the person experiences no choice;
7. Contain no sentences which violate the semantic conditions of wellformedness.

(Quoted from *Structure of Magic I*, Bandler & Grinder 1975)

META MODEL™
DELETION
INFORMATION GATHERING

Simple Deletion:
Statement with missing or deficient information.

Comparative Deletion:
Missing standard of evaluation.

Lack of Referential Index:
Unidentified pronoun.

Unspecified Verb:
Verbs that delete specifics about How, When, Where.

META MODEL™
DISTORTION
SEMANTIC ILL-FORMEDNESS

Nominalization:
Verb made into a noun (thing or event) thus obscuring the process or action.

Cause/Effect:
A specific stimulus causes a specific experience. $X \rightarrow Y$

Mind Reading:
Assuming you know what the other person thinks, feels, etc.

Complex Equivalence:
Conclusion based on belief that outcome will always be the same. $X = Y$

Lost Performative:
Value judgments or opinions in which the source of assertion is missing.

META MODEL™
GENERALIZATION
LIMITS OF THE SPEAKER'S MODEL

Universal Quantifiers:
Generalizations that preclude exceptions or alternative choices.

Modal Operators of Necessity/Possibility:
Words that require particular action or imply no choice.

Presuppositions:
Something implicitly required in order to understand a sentence.

META MODEL™

Surface Structure

Deep Structure

E X P E R I E N C E

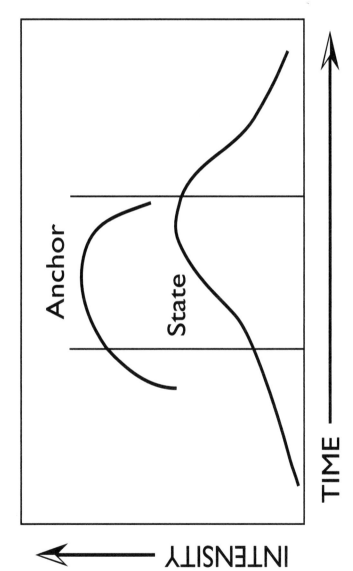

ANCHORING
INSTALLATION OF AN ANCHOR

Anchor

State

INTENSITY

TIME

Meta Publications
P.O. Box 1910
Capitola, CA 95010
Phone: (408) 464-0254
FAX: (408) 464-0517

To contact Richard Bandler:
44 Montgomery St. 5th Floor
San Francisco, CA 94104
Phone: (415) 955-0541
FAX: (415) 955-0542

To Contact John La Valle:
P.O. Box 828
Hopatcong, NJ 07843
Phone: (201) 770-3600
FAX: (201) 770-0314

𝕿𝖍𝖊 𝕾𝖔𝖈𝖎𝖊𝖙𝖞 𝖔𝖋
𝕹𝖊𝖚𝖗𝖔-𝕷𝖎𝖓𝖌𝖚𝖎𝖘𝖙𝖎𝖈 𝕻𝖗𝖔𝖌𝖗𝖆𝖒𝖒𝖎𝖓𝖌™

Established in 1978, the Society of Neuro-Linguistic Programming™ is a worldwide organization set up for the purpose of exerting quality control over those training programs and services claiming to represent the model of Neuro-Linguistic Programming™ (NLP). The seal above indicates Society Certification and is usually advertised by Society approved institutes and centers. We highly recommend that you exercise caution as you apply the techniques and skills of NLP. We also urge you to attend only those seminars, workshops and training programs that been officially designed and certified by The Society of Neuro-Linguistic Programming™. Any training programs that have been approved and endorsed by The Society of Neuro-Linguistic Programming™ will display a copy of the registered certification mark(s) of the Society of Neuro-Linguistic Programming™. The Society of Neuro-Linguistic Programming™ is set up for the purpose of exerting quality control over those training programs, services and materials claiming to represent the model of Neuro-Linguistic Programming™.

As a protection for you and for those around you, The Society of NLP™ requires participants to sign licensing agreements which guarantees that those certified and licensed in this technology will use it with the highest integrity. It is also a way to insure that all the trainings you attend are of the highest quality and that your trainers are updated and current with the constant evolution of the field of Neuro-Linguistic Programming™ and Design Human Engineering™.

There are four levels of certification and licensing granted by The Society of Neuro-Linguistic Programming™: Practitioner, Master Practitioner, Trainer and Master Trainer. All certificates issued by The Society of Neuro-Linguistic Programming™, the Society seal, and Richard Bandler's signature in penned ink. Trainers may train Practitioners and Master Practitioners who then may get certified and licensed by Richard Bandler and The Society of Neuro-Linguistic Programming™. Master Trainer is a level recognized because of special circumstances and contributions. This level is reserved and can only be granted by Richard Bandler and The Society of Neuro-Linguistic Programming™. Master Trainers may not certify Trainers except under special written permission of Dr. Bandler.

Design Human Engineering™ (DHE) may only be trained by Trainers of DHE. This level of certification is granted only by Richard Bandler and The Society of Neuro-Linguistic Programming™. Their certificate will specifically state "Trainer of Design Human Engineering™" with the Society Seal and Richard Bandler's signature.

To be sure you are purchasing Pure NLP products and/or services, please call the Society of Neuro-Linguistic Programming™. We are most interested in protecting the technology's integrity. All certifications and licensing carry a two (2) year expiration date, the Society Seal, and Richard Bandler's signature. You have the right to ask anyone advertising NLP services to show you their license and/or certification. An inability to produce this document may one of two possibilities: either the person and/or organization is defrauding the public, or they have been defrauded themselves by another organization purporting to be a certifying organization. Under either condition, please notify The Society of Neuro-Linguistic Programming™ so that we may take steps to rectify the situation.

Each license and/or certification has a two year expiration date. This is because the technology is constantly evolving and Dr. Bandler is continuing his development contributions to human evolution. The Society expects that those who hold certification continually update their skills and renew their certifications and/or licenses. Renewal is not automatic and is easy. Do not accept certifications and/or licenses without expiration dates. If you have benefited from Richard's contributions in the form of the technologies he has developed, we appreciate it when you help us to point out the charlatans who are out there misinforming the public. This is more of a moral issue than anything else. Richard and the Society are interested in people doing the right things and becoming very prosperous in all areas of their lives. There is an unlimited amount of opportunity for everyone. There is no need to steal.

If you are certified at any level of Design Human Engineering™, you must obtain express written permission for each usage of the term or symbol (DHE™) from Richard Bandler. This can be obtained by contacting the First Institute of NLP™ and DHE™ at (415) 955-0541 or 44 Montgomery St., 5th floor, San Francisco, Ca. 94104. Each use of the term Design Human Engineering™ must be earmarked with a (™) as well as a symbol that refers to the phrase "Design Human Engineering™ and DHE™ is used with express written permission of Richard Bandler."

ONLY RICHARD BANDLER, PERSONALLY, MAY TRAIN TRAINERS OF NLP™, except under express written permission from Richard Bandler.

Should you be a member of the Society of Neuro-Linguistic Programming™ and have not complied with the above requirements, we wish to make you aware that you may grandfather your trainees for a limited time.

The Society publishes its directory of members in good standing and is happy to provide referrals upon request and encourages participation in this opportunity to make a difference for everyone.